WITH WELLINGTON
IN THE PENINSULA

WITH WELLINGTON IN THE PENINSULA

*The Adventures of
a Highland Soldier, 1808–1814*

Edited by Paul Cowan

Frontline Books, London

With Wellington in the Peninsula: The Adventures of a Highland Soldier, 1808–1814
First published in 2015 by Frontline Books,
an imprint of Pen & Sword Books Ltd,
47 Church Street, Barnsley, S.Yorkshire, S70 2AS
www.frontline-books.com

Edited text, Introduction and Commentary © Paul Cowan, 2015

The right of Paul Cowan to be identified as the author of this work has been
asserted by him in accordance with the Copyright, Designs and Patents Act 1988.

ISBN: 978-1-84832-786-3

CIP data records for this title are available from the British Library

For more information on our books, please visit
www.frontline-books.com, email info@frontline-books.com
or write to us at the above address.

Printed and bound by CPI Group (UK) Ltd, Croydon, CR0 4YY

Typeset in Palatino by MATS, Leigh-on-Sea, Essex

Contents

Place of Birth – A Liquorish Cook – Highland Method of
Stopping a Leak – Cork to Mondego Bay – Portugueze
Hospitality – Battle of Roleia – Death Scenes – Battle
of Vimiera – Presentiment of Death – General Brennier –
A Bloody Aide de Camp – Corporal Mackay Exposed –
A Trouble-breeding Sword – French Temerity – A Change
of Linen – Wellesley's Encomiums – British Folly – March
to Lisbon – A Jolly Priest – Tartan Cullottes – Ostrich Feathers –
Foreign Deserters – Strong Italian.

A Circuitous March from Lisbon to Corunna – Including,
Superstition – Behaviour of Spaniards – Clerical Civility –
Escurial – War of Words – The Unfortunate Equestrian –
A Treat – Hypocrisy – Commissary-guard Miseries –
The Disastrous Retreat – Labour in Vain – Skirmish at Lugo –
Mendicant Officers – A Happy Discovery – Horrors –

Contents

The Deserted House – Honey versus Bread – A Gallant
Action – A Bright Prospect – Battle of Corunna – A Pell-Mell
Embarkation.

Adventure – Removal to Barba – Portugueze Customs,
Opinions, Recruits, and Gullibility – A Hot March
to Portalegre.

CONTENTS

Much Ado about Nothing – Winter Quarters in Ort – A Muddy Story – French Gun-boats – A Romantic Story – Climate.

Illustrations

Maps

Introduction

When this book was first published in 1827, as *Vicissitudes in the Life of a Scottish Soldier*, it was one of the first military memoirs to attempt to paint a realistic picture of the Peninsular War as seen through the eyes of a member of the rank and file. Though laced with humour and anecdote, the book also pulled no punches when it came to describing the lot of a private in Wellington's Army.

For the book's anonymous narrator, soldiering was a job and not always a pleasant one. He fought who he was told to, where he was told to. He even goes so far as to question what business he and his comrades in the 71st Highland Regiment of Light Infantry had in Portugal, Spain or France. For example, he describes the liberation of Portugal as 'a plausible pretext for murder' and confesses that in Spain the local people obviously regarded the British as 'uninvited intruders'. Nor does he spare his readers the horrors of his chosen trade. He talks of standing in the ranks watching wounded men nearby struggling in vain to escape a grass fire. Readers are also reminded that he and his comrades were not infrequently vermin-ridden, half-starved and clothed in rags. The narrator laments the order to retreat from the Madrid area in 1808. 'This word [order] strongly reminded us that we were not travelling either for

1

instruction or amusement, that we had no will of our own, and, in short, that we were slaves, that must be killed, or starve, or perish with cold, or walk to the end of the world if commanded,' he reflects early on in the book.

And despite the doubly elite status of the 71st as both a Highland and a light infantry unit, the narrator confesses that he and his comrades were not always willing warriors. This, according to him, was particularly true when the war moved into the Pyrenees. 'This continual mountain-warfare harassed us to a considerable degree; so much so, indeed, that death itself was eagerly panted for by many; others had serious thoughts about allowing themselves to fall into enemy hands,' he admits. The disastrous, from the 71st's point of view, Battle of Vitoria in June 1813, when combined with the miseries of the Pyrenees, would appear to have taken the fighting edge off the battalion. The narrator notes: 'the fact is, fighting had begun to lose its novelty'.

Such comments did not endear the book to some reviewers when it was published. That bastion of Tory privilege within the armed forces *The Military and Naval Magazine* went so far as to brand the book 'trash'. The narrator's unabashed criticisms of his superiors, both commissioned and non-commissioned, also attracted the ire of the *Literary Gazette and Journal of Belles Lettres*. It could be argued that the book's attempt to create an honest account of war was ahead of its time. The narrator makes no apologies for failing to give an overall account of the battles he fought in and argues that a private soldier's view of the action often went no further than the distance of a stone's throw: 'Such being the case, I will confine myself chiefly to what came under my own immediate observation; which I dare say will satisfy the reader better than if I made up my narrative from gazettes, or stolen from others.'

Vicissitudes in the Life of a Scottish Soldier frankly acknowledged its debt to a bestseller called *Journal of a Soldier of the 71st,* which had been published in 1819. The narrator of *Vicissitudes* appears to have consciously decided against repeating many of the anecdotes that appeared in *Journal of a Soldier,* though the incidents recounted would have been well known to anyone who served with the regiment. This means the two books complement each other and between them give a fuller picture of one battalion's war than is available for most units in Wellington's Army.

Some excellent detective work by historian and author Stuart Reid recently revealed that Thomas, the narrator of *Journal of a Soldier,* was based on the experiences of at least three members of the 71st. Ghostwriter John Howell's rather precious and sometimes sneering creation Thomas perhaps had more in common with his readers than with the rank and file. The narrator of *Vicissitudes* has no such pretensions of gentility. He is unashamedly a working man who takes coarse delight in his tales of sneaking, or as he terms it 'progging', food and alcohol at every opportunity. He admires the carrying capacity of the kilt aprons worn by members of the 92nd Gordon Highlanders when they loot bread. The supposed foolishness of his fellow soldiers, especially Highlanders and Irishmen, provides much fodder for derisive comment.

Vicissitudes, like *Journal of a Soldier,* hid behind an anonymous author. This has to raise the question of its authenticity as an account of the Peninsular War. Fortunately, three other first-person accounts written by members of the 71st which came to light many decades after *Vicissitudes* was published corroborate much of what appears in it. As none of the accounts was intended for publication, it is unlikely that John Mcfarlane, William Gavin or Balfour Kermack raided *Vicissitudes* for material. But the eyewitness accounts they provide vary just enough from *Vicissitudes* to rule all three out as the book's narrator. The formal histories of the 71st are less valuable when it comes to corroborating *Vicissitudes.* They appear to lean heavily on both *Vicissitudes* and *Journal of a Soldier* but do not always credit them as sources.

The London publishers of *Vicissitudes* strongly believed there was a public appetite for a second memoir from a ranker who served with the much-storied 71st during the Peninsular War. The regiment's exploits at the Battle of Vimeiro in 1808 had been the subject of a number of prints and even a commemorative jug. It was at Vimeiro that the 71st captured themselves a French general, and Piper George Clark played his comrades into action despite being badly wounded. A similar exploit in India in 1897 by Piper George Findlater of the Gordon Highlanders earned him a Victoria Cross. Both Piper Clark's exploit and the capture of the French officer were the subjects of several mass-produced engravings. Our author vigorously challenges the long accepted version of the latter incident.

The 71st had been involved in some of the hardest fought battles of both the 1808–09 and 1810–14 Peninsular War campaigns. The 71st had even managed to earn the praise of members of other regiments. Sergeant John Donaldson of the 94th Scotch Brigade fought alongside the 71st at Fuentes de Onoro and noted in his memoirs that the regiment was 'always remarkable for its gallantry'. Captain John Patterson's 50th Foot was brigaded with the 71st from 1810 onwards, and he refers to the Scots battalion as 'the gallant 71st'. The 71st's fine reputation predated the Peninsular War. In 1800 it was one of just over a dozen regiments asked to supply a detachment for an experimental rifle unit. That unit was formalised as the Rifle Corps, later to become the 95th Regiment and then the Rifle Brigade. The 71st contributed thirty-two of the first riflemen.

The 92nd Gordon Highlanders were brigaded with the 71st and 50th West Kents but its historians do not single their Scottish colleagues out for much praise. In fact, there seems to have been tension between the two Scots units. The 71st were second only in seniority among the Highland regiments to the 42nd Royal Highlanders, better known as the Black Watch. The regiment had first paraded as the 73rd McLeod Highlanders in 1778 before being sent to India. But jealousy over seniority was probably not at the root of the bad feeling between the two Highland regiments. In 1800 the 71st could still claim to contain around 600 'true' Highlanders, but around that time it was stationed in Ireland where many men from the Scottish home defence fencible regiments transferred to its ranks. Many of the former fencibles had fought against Irish rebels and were members of the virulently anti-Catholic Orange Order. The 92nd was in part recruited from the Catholic clans of western Inverness-shire.

The 71st lacked the landlord patronage in the north and west of Scotland to compete for recruits with the plethora of Highland regiments raised to fight Napoleon's legions. A son sent into the army could often mean a new or improved tenancy agreement for an impoverished Highland family. Conversely, refusal might cost parents dear. The estimate by the narrator of *Vicissitudes* that there were only forty or fifty Gaelic speakers with the 71st at the Battle of Fuentes de Onoro in 1811 is, judging from the not always accurate regimental records, probably not too far from the mark.

But while the 71st did not include as many Gaelic speakers as the more junior Highland regiments, such as the Camerons, Ross-shire Buffs, Gordons or Argylls, it was at least a Scottish regiment. In 1809 six regiments were deprived of their Highland status as English and Irish recruits predominated in their ranks. Throughout the Peninsular War the national balance within the 71st appears to have remained fairly constant at approximately 65 per cent Scottish, 28 per cent Irish and 7 per cent English. Some commanders believed that a mix of nationalities was desirable as it made a battalion more resilient. This is reflected in the commanding officer of the 2nd Battalion of the 28th Foot, the North Gloucestershire Regiment, making a plea in 1807 to Whitehall for a substantial draft of men from the various Scottish home defence units.

The age of the recruits to the 71st, late teens or early 20s, mirrored those entering most of Wellington's infantry battalions. The youngest recruit to the 71st would seem to have been twelve-and-a-half-year-old John Groves from Dumfries-shire. Sergeant John West from Cork was reported to have been 64 years old when he was discharged in 1812 after ten years with the 71st. He had been soldiering since 1761. The regiment also included a sprinkling of men in their 30s and late 40s. By modern standards recruits to the 71st were on the short side but typical of one of Wellington's battalions, with two-thirds of them being under 5ft 8in tall. The less than a dozen recruits from continental Europe seem to have been taller, with three of them 6ft tall or more. The 71st had almost twice as many ex-weavers in its ranks than would be expected in a typical infantry battalion, at approximately 40 per cent of recruits. This probably reflects employment patterns in Scotland and the cyclical nature of the textile industry. The next largest trade on enlistment was labourer at just short of 40 per cent. Weavers and labourers therefore made up around 80 per cent of recruits and other trades were a long way behind. Shoemakers were the next biggest grouping at around 3.5 per cent, with tailors not far behind. The regiment also attracted a sprinkling of black-smiths, stone masons, carpenters, sailors and cotton spinners. There was at least one former schoolteacher, a silversmith, a gunsmith, a bookbinder and a watchmaker.

Sickness levels in Wellington's Army, usually regarded as a good indicator of unit morale, often ran at 25 per cent of a battalion's strength. When the 71st sailed for Portugal in 1808 there were 134 men on the sick roll, which works out at 15 per cent of strength. At the end of the war in 1814 there were 181 men reporting sick, or 21 per cent of strength. Another indication of unit morale is the desertion rate. In 1811 the 71st reported only three desertions. That same year the 50th had three and the 92nd Gordon Highlanders one. The average figure for an infantry or cavalry unit in 1811 was ten deserters. The 71st reported around 100 men dead in 1811. Two other battalions which suffered similar losses that year, the 74th Foot, later the 2nd Battalion of the Highland Light Infantry, and the 94th Scotch Brigade reported sixty-one and thirty-three deserters respectively.

The regiment went into action in 1808 in uniforms which left little doubt it was a Highland unit. It had switched from kilts to tartan trews in 1806 but kept its distinctive ostrich-feather bonnets. Conversion to light infantry status three years later led to another change of uniform for the 71st and a struggle to retain any sign of Scottishness. Eventually, it was agreed that the regiment could retain its kilted pipers and Highland bonnets. The bonnets soon shed their feathers and were blocked up to resemble a standard issue infantry shako. But the headgear retained the red and white diced band around its base. By the time of Waterloo, green squares had been added to the dicing.

Permission to retain 'such portions of the national dress as might not be inconsistent with their duties as a light corps' leads some commentators to believe the 71st returned to Portugal in 1810 wearing trews. But they speculate that a shortage of tartan cloth meant that as the trews wore out they were replaced with standard-issue grey trousers. The regiment went back into trews in the late 1820s and declined War Office offers in 1875, 1877 and 1881 to have the kilt restored. The regiment's leadership changed its mind when the Scottish Lowland regiments adopted trews after 1881 but it was 1947 before the Highland Light Infantry became a kilted unit again. The kilts were lost in 1959 when the HLI merged with the Royal Scots Fusiliers to form the Royal Highland Fusiliers. The 2006 transformation of the RHF into the 2nd Battalion of the Royal Regiment of Scotland saw the kilts restored yet again.

One of the reasons given by the narrator of *Vicissitudes* for joining the 71st was that it contained a number of men from his home city of Glasgow. While he seems to come through the fighting unscathed, it may be instructive to consider the fate of some of his Glaswegian contemporaries. A check of fifty-six discharges granted to Glasgow-born men showed thirty-four of them had been wounded at least once. The disastrous fighting on the Heights of Puebla during the 1813 Battle of Vitoria ended the military careers of Gavin Forrester, James McGrigor, John McNee, Walter Handiside, James Fraser, Walter McFate and Bugler George Nelson; all were pensioned off due to serious wounds. John Kelloch was also pensioned off as a result of a knee wound suffered at Vitoria but managed to re-enlist in the 70th Foot in 1815. Bugler John Mcfarlane and Sergeant William Carmichael were also wounded at Vitoria but managed to remain with the regiment. John Donaldson was wounded at Maya in July 1813 in fighting that cost John McVicar an arm. Donaldson was to be wounded again at Waterloo in 1815. Vitoria inflicted so many casualties, around 400 dead, wounded and missing, that the regimental clerks ran out of printed discharge forms and had to produce them by hand.

Bugler William Glenn survived the war only to fall victim to a purge of the regiment before it returned from occupation duties in France in 1819 which was intended to reduce its establishment to peacetime levels. He was discharged for being undersized, he was 5ft 3in, and for being unsatisfactory as a bugler. As Glenn had been with the 71st since 1806, the army had taken its time in recognising his shortcomings.

Hugh McLean would appear to have been another victim of the purge. His character on discharge was given as 'very bad' and noted he had been 'repeatedly brought before regimental court martial' during his almost thirteen years with the 71st. With Napoleon exiled to the mid-Atlantic island of St. Helena, the army decided it could finally dispense with McLean's services. Corporal William Mason, still carrying the scars from the day he was hacked around the head by a French sabre at Arroyo dos Molinos in 1811, survived the cull but was discharged a year later as 'worn out'. His character was given as 'steady, regular and brave'.

So much for some of the narrator's Glasgow contemporaries in the 71st, but what of the man himself? Sadly, the 71st were happier with muskets in their hands than staining their fingers with pen and ink. The regimental records are often incomplete and inconsistent. Men appear on the muster rolls who fail to be recorded in the description books for either the 1st Battalion or its feeder 2nd Battalion. Pension records are also inconsistent when it comes to detail. It sometimes appears that, much as in the French Foreign Legion, a recruit was who he said he was, few questions were asked and the details could be changed at a later date. By adopting a cloak of anonymity the narrator could afford to be more candid and scurrilous than if he had put his name to his story. Sergeant Joseph Donaldson in his book about his time with the 94th Scotch Brigade originally identified himself in the first edition only as James. But is there something more to the reluctance of the narrator of *Vicissitudes* to identify himself?

The narrator has very little to say about himself other than he was from Glasgow and had served in several units before joining the 71st around the time of its return from South America in 1807. Only one man appears in the description books and the pension records who meets all three criteria. Glasgow-born Alex Brice, or Bryce, joined the 71st in February 1807 at Fort George near Inverness where he had been serving with the 6th Royal Veterans. He had also served with the North Lowland Fencibles and served two years in the 71st between 1800 and 1802 when he rose to the rank of corporal. He also appears to share the narrator's experience of being on the sick roll after the Walcheren Campaign of 1809. As the 1st Battalion did not return from

South America until late in 1807, Brice's enlistment is also recorded in the 2nd Battalion's description book. The date of his transfer from the 2nd Battalion to the 1st Battalion is given as 22 May 1809 – almost a year after the book begins with the 71st's landing in Portugal. However, the vast majority of transfers between the battalions supposedly took place on 22 May 1809 and it seems this date may well be an administrative fiction – especially as the book purports to cover the period 1810–20.

A second discrepancy is more troubling. Alex Brice was discharged from the 71st in 1813 and the book's narrative continues up until the regiment's return from France in August 1814. Did someone else take up the story? Adam Brice had served with the 71st since 1806. In his discharge papers his place of birth is listed as Glasgow. The description book has no Adam Brice from Glasgow but it does have a Stirling man called Adam Brice. His physical description is virtually identical to the man in the discharge document. His discharge date is exactly the same – 6 August 1816. Alex, when he was discharged, headed not for Glasgow but for Stirling. Could Adam and Alex have been close relatives, brothers even? Adam eventually surrendered his pension rights and used the lump sum he received to emigrate to Canada. It may be no coincidence that perhaps the only copy of *Vicissitudes* not held by a national or major academic library surfaced in the Canadian province of Ontario in 2003.

The Stirling connection may be significant for another reason. Most Napoleonic memoirs which purport to have been written by a member of the rank and file involved a ghostwriter, sometimes a former officer. One of the most prolific of the military ghostwriters of the period was George Robert Gleig, a former officer in the 85th Foot who was brought up in the Stirling area. The British Library credits Gleig with thirty-six books from eleven publishers. He regularly wrote for the same publisher who brought out

Vicissitudes – Henry Colbourn. He was interviewing army pensioners for a book to be published by Colbourn around the time *Vicissitudes* was written. Stylistically, *Vicissitudes* is very similar to some of Gleig's known work, including his fondness for references to literature and Greek mythology. He also, but not always, preferred the spelling 'trowsers' favoured in *Vicissitudes* and the already archaic 'overplus' for extra or surplus.

There can be little doubt that *Vicissitudes in the Life of a Scottish Soldier* is an authentic account of one of Wellington's crack battalions at war. Certainly the regiment's own historians and that respected chronicler of the Peninsular War, Sir Charles Oman, believed it was a genuine eyewitness account. Does the possibility that it may be based on two eyewitnesses rather than one make it any less vivid or compelling?

Paul Cowan,
Alberta,
Canada,
2015

11

Note on Text and Maps

The original spelling has been retained as far as possible. Where the original spelling could be mistaken for a modern misprint, for example 'corse' for 'corpse', it has been updated. The maps were specially commissioned and are based on contemporary maps and accounts.

Original 1827 Editor's Advertisement

We possess many works which present all the grand and general features of our Continental campaigns; but we know very little about the minuter details that gave the Peninsular war its peculiar character and colouring. The courage of our soldiers, their consistency under daily sufferings and privations, their kindness to the foreigners they were protecting, and their generosity to the foe they opposed, have been lauded, in the aggregate, both in prose and rhyme; but there are few traits preserved of the individual prowess and individual adventure, – of the light-heartedness, the misery, the ludicrous or lamentable incidents, the vices that diversify the life and character of a private soldier. The single subject here selected for a picture will, in the main points, illustrate the personal condition of the whole of our army; and, from such a story, many particulars may be learned regarding the conduct of the officers engaged in the Peninsular war, which could in no other way be obtained; for the commanders would hardly be vain enough to chronicle their own acts of generosity, – and they might be withheld by shame, and their historians by delicacy, from speaking of the deeds of despotism and cruelty in which it is known that some of them have occasionally indulged.

On these accounts, therefore the VICISSITUDES in the LIFE of our SCOTTISH SOLDIER will, no doubt, be perused with interest, – an interest which will be no means diminished by the publication of the fact that he belonged to the 71st Regiment, – one of the most gallant in the service, and one from which there has already emanated a similar narrative, which has excited no small proportion of public attention and applause.

VICISSITUDES
IN THE
LIFE OF A SCOTTISH SOLDIER

FIRST PENINSULAR
CAMPAIGN
1808-1809

Corunna
(1809)

Lugo

Astorga

Sahagun

Mayorga

Benavente

Spain

Oporto

Salamanca

Guadarrama

Escorial

Mondego
Bay

Figueira

Alcobaca

Talavera

Almaraz

Rolica
(1808)

Vimeiro
(1808)

Torres Vedras

Lisbon

Badajoz

Portugal

N

Chapter One

The reader of this work can have little interest in knowing my name, and therefore I have suppressed it altogether. It is sufficient to say, that I was born in the city of Glasgow; enlisted at the age of sixteen; passed through the usual routine of a soldier's life in the three kingdoms; and, after being in more than one corps, I eventually entered the 71st, or Glasgow regiment,[1] when it had just arrived from South America.[2] The very name of this corps, and its containing so many of my townsmen and acquaintances, will account for my desire to belong to it.

In the year 1808 we were lying at Cork along with the army forming there under the command of Sir Arthur Wellesley.[3] It was on the 5th of June that we embarked, totally ignorant of the place of our destination. It is true,

---

[1] At this time the 71st was known as the Glasgow Highland Regiment.
[2] The regiment was part of the disastrous 1806 attack on the Spanish-held city of Buenos Aires in South America. After capturing the city, they were overwhelmed when the city's population staged a rising as Spanish troops approached. The battalion was imprisoned and did not return to the United Kingdom until December 1807. A total of ninety-six men opted to remain in Argentina.
[3] Later the Duke of Wellington. Arthur Wellesley had made his reputation in India. He began his military career with the 73rd

there were many surmises afloat, such as, that we were going to America,[4] and so forth. But after all, we lay snug in the Cove of Cork for about five weeks; during the whole of which time, the whole deck of the vessel that I was in, was a continual scene of uproar and jovial mirth. Every afternoon the piper played his best reel-tunes, to which the men danced with high glee; liquor was also very plentifully handed about. This was chiefly owing to the settlement of a long arrears of pay due to the soldiers, who had arrived from America.[5] Our vessel, the *Plantagenet*, belonged to Kirkcaldy, or, at any rate, the crew were all natives of that place. They had, like other Scotch vessels, always a liberal allowance of kale: their old greasy cook, like the rest of his trade, being fonder of drink than of meat, was constantly going on deck, offering to 'gie a ladlefu' o' kail for a drappy o' drink'. One day we were ordered ashore to be inspected. The small boat that I was in being leaky, one of the men (a Highlander) thinking, it seems, to rectify this defect, suddenly pulled a plug out, and the water, of course, rushed in upon us in great quantities. The author of this misfortune had not the presence of mind which one of his countrymen had when in a similar predicament; this was, to thrust his thumb into the hole and cut it off. Fortunately we were near the shore, or

---

(Highland) Foot in March 1787 but transferred to another regiment nine months later. His brother Richard effectively, through a large loan, bought him command of the 33rd (1st Yorkshire West Riding and later the Duke of Wellington's) Foot in 1793.

[4] The expeditionary force assembling at Cork was initially earmarked for an invasion of the Spanish colonies in South America.

[5] The veterans of the Buenos Aires campaign were awarded prize money related to the seizure of one million gold dollars from the Argentinian treasury. Privates received £18 6s 0d. On the regiment's return from imprisonment, it was stationed at Middleton Barracks near Cork in Ireland. One soldier later recounted that for eight days the barracks were ankle deep in beer and whisky as the soldiers spent their windfall.

the most tragical consequences might have taken place. On questioning the Highlandman, his only excuse was, 'that he thought to let water out!'

At length, on the 12th of July, the fleet put out to sea; it consisted of seventy transports, two men of war, and a gunbrig, the whole containing about 10,000 troops. While the land was receding from our view, every deck was covered by the men taking a last look at Ireland. At a time like this, when one's country is diminishing into a speck upon the waters, even the most careless are thoughtful. An ordinary passenger has only the dangers of the sea and climate to fear; but the soldier has, in addition, those of war; he feels a certainty that, among the numbers around him, many will never return, – 'and who knows', he thinks to himself, 'but I may be one of them?' But our reflections soon began to be sadly disturbed; present misery alone engrossed the attention of all; for a stiff though favourable breeze had sprung up, which in a short time threw nearly the whole of our men into the pains of sea-sickness. Out of 250 on board, perhaps there were not above a dozen of us that could stand upright, or, in other words, were well. Happily for me, I was among the latter number. In fact I never felt this complaint in the slightest degree, and was, of course, a little surprised to see so many in a terrible state who had even twice crossed the line.[6] In a *gourmand's* eyes, I was a happy man that day; the mess I belonged to consisted of six men, but as they were all sick except myself, the whole of their provisions and rum fell to my share; and the value of this was considerably enhanced on account of its being pudding-day.

Nothing particular occurred during the rest of the voyage. We passed swiftly through the Bay of Biscay, saw Cape Finisterre in Spain; and after a passage of fourteen days, our fleet dropped their anchors in Mondego Bay.[7] We rode at

---

[6] The Equator.
[7] About 100 miles north of Lisbon.

anchor for some days, during which time a heavy swell prevailed through the bay, and which made the vessels pitch and roll in a very disagreeable manner. The difficulty of walking on the deck was increased by the old cook's slush, or grease barrel, being overturned by accident. Previous to our landing everyone was busily engaged in cleaning himself from the dirt inseparable from a crowded transport. The coming of the 3rd of August saw us in the boats, leaving the old *Plantagenet* without a tear. As we approached the beach, crowds of Portugueze welcomed us by repeated acclamations; and no sooner had we leaped on the peninsular shore, than a number of women came down, and distributed fruit among us in great abundance: each of them had her apron loaded. Having nothing ready to put fruit in, I took off my bonnet; scarcely had I done so, when it was filled to the head, – legions of hands striving with one another to get something in. After remaining a short time on the beach, we crossed the river Mondego in Portugueze boats, and then commenced our march. Here, for the first time I believe, the shores of Portugal resounded with the yell of a Scottish bagpipe. A foretaste of cam-paigning miseries now began; the day was insufferably hot; no water could be had, our fatigue and thirst were also increased by being obliged to wade through the burning sands of the coast.[8] Two leagues were gone over, when the order to halt was given. Rejoiced at the news, I threw myself under the shade of a tree, and soon fell into a comfortable nap. On awakening, I found myself in a tented field, a number of men having been employed in erecting a canvas city. We remained some days encamped, waiting till the stores were landed.

On the 10th we advanced up country: on the 14th the advanced guard of our army had a skirmish with the French.

---

[8] Four members of the regiment died from thirst or heat exhaustion while marching from Mondego Bay.

In the course of this march, we began to get rather sceptical in our belief of the Portugueze being so overjoyed and grateful for the interference of the British. As we passed through the village of Alcobaca, an old blind woman stood on a hillock, bawling with all her might 'Viva los Francesos!' On hearing this, another woman went up and whispered into her ear; instantly she began to call out as lustily as before, 'Viva los Ingles!' She evidently had taken us for Frenchmen, till warned of the mistake; but the adulation was then too common, or rather too late for us to swallow. Perhaps the sentiments of the whole nation with regard to us, might have been gained from this old lady: armed foreigners, although they have friendly intentions, are always to be distrusted.

It was not until the 16th that I first beheld the French; they were posted on the heights of Roleia.[9] Here I could not but reflect, that these men are what is called our 'hereditary enemies'. How false is that name! What quarrel had we with the party opposite us? What injury had they done to us? They had unjustly subdued the Portugueze – but that was no business of ours. To give liberty to an oppressed nation we were come; yes, this is a most plausible pretext for murder.

But to the point. Preparations were now made to drive the enemy from their situation; part of our army advanced to the attack, the light company of our regiment accompanied the attacking party. I was, with the rest of the regiment, stationary. The engagement now commenced, but we could only see at a distance the 'tug of war'. The incessant discharge of musketry, and the smoke and roar of the artillery, completed the effect: occasionally, however, a stray cannonball from the French would whistle over our heads, and sink with a heavy sound into the earth. One of these formidable missiles struck off an artilleryman's leg, close by us. This was

---

[9] Also spelled Roliça. The 71st reported one man killed and one wounded in the battle.

sufficient to remind us, that even where we were, safety was out of the question. The most part of the day we were tormented with thirst, although there was no want of springs around us. The reason for this was, that some of our men, while hot and fatigued, had drunk the water, which naturally causing, in their state, a disagreeable effect, reports were immediately spread, that the French had poisoned the water. We were young enough warriors to believe this, and consequently did not dare to touch a drop.

The enemy having commenced a retreat, we were ordered to advance. While marching up the road, I passed over the dead body of a young Swiss soldier, his red clothing allowing us to know his nation. He had received a ball in the middle of the forehead. This was the first victim to the deity of war I had yet seen, but, as we advanced, many more met our sight. The road and contiguous fields were literally covered with dead and dying, both British and French. The horror of the scene was increased in consequence of the hedges and long grass taking fire. We had to endure the appalling view of the impotent efforts of several poor wounded wretches endeavouring to drag themselves from the devouring flames: there was no time to render them assistance; besides, self-preservation warned us that danger was to be apprehended from the fire communicating with our cartridge boxes. After reaching the summit of the heights, there was nothing to do but look at the French filing off in columns. Thus concluded the battle of Roleia.

The French were only 6,000 strong: our army was much superior in number,[10] although not all engaged. Upon the whole, therefore, there was no great reason for us to boast. We gained our point by compelling the enemy to quit the

---

[10] Estimates of the size of the two armies vary. The number of French troops engaged is usually estimated at between 4,000 and 5,000 men, while Wellesley's British-Portuguese army is believed to have been 15,000 strong.

heights; but they effected this in good order. Next morning we marched to the village of Vimiera,[11] and encamped in its environs for two days. Here the army was joined by reinforcements under General Anstruther;[12] they had landed in Peniche Bay.

The 21st of August, 1808, was destined to be a memorable day – at least so far as the death of thousands could make it so. It was a Sunday; we had been ordered to attend divine service in the morning, and were accordingly preparing ourselves for this, when the drum of the 40th regiment[13] beating to arms, gave a general alarm. On hearing the clamour, Colonel Pack[14] came out of his tent and ordered us to fall in, as the enemy were advancing to the attack. We then marched, and took up a position on a rising ground to the left of our army; thus, contrary to expectation, we found ourselves about to enter into a service totally different to that which was at first intended. The battle had by this time commenced on the right; consequently, as at Roleia, we were obliged to stand for a while exposed to a distant cannonade. A shell also fell and burst near our company; one of the splinters wounded a man severely, who stood third from me on the left. A party of officers went out one at a time, a short distance from us, in order to obtain a closer view of the engagement; one of them, belonging to the

---

[11] There are several versions of this name. The official British battle honour is Vimiera, the modern Portuguese spelling is Vimeiro while some British historians spell it Vimiero.

[12] Major General Robert Anstruther. After sterling service in Egypt and at Vimeiro, he died from exhaustion at Corunna.

[13] The 40th (2nd Somerset) Foot.

[14] Lieutenant Colonel Denis Pack, Irish-born commander of the 71st. He commanded the regiment during the seizure of the Cape of Good Hope in South Africa from the Dutch in 1805 and the ill-fated Buenos Aires campaign. He was taken prisoner in Argentina but escaped. He later commanded a Portuguese brigade in the Peninsular War and a British brigade at the Battle of Waterloo in 1815. He died in 1823.

82nd,[15] fell dead in our sight: slain, strange to say, by the mere wind of a cannon-ball; not a scratch being on his body. The balls were now flying so thick, that we received orders to sit down: even in this position, they would ever and anon rattle through among the fixed bayonets, and descend so low as to knock the bonnets off our heads! We remained in this tantalizing state for some time, really envying our comrades on the right, who had the opportunity of revenging themselves; truly the situation we were then placed in is the most trying for the soldier's courage. He feels himself indescribable terror, which is entirely unknown when once he has fairly entered the hottest part of an engagement.

At length we beheld, with great satisfaction, the enemy advancing towards us.[16] We then stood to our arms, our flank files ran out to skirmish, but they were soon driven in again by the steady approach of the French. I now had the opportunity to see them face to face; they differed widely from us in dress in this instance, being all clothed in long white smock-frocks and trowsers, and having hairy knapsacks hanging loosely on their backs. But little time was left for observation, on account of General Ferguson[17] riding up to the __th,[18] which lay close beside us, and ordering that

---

[15] The 82nd (Prince of Wales's Volunteers) Foot.

[16] The 71st had been sent to block a French attempt to outflank Wellesley's army.

[17] Major General Ronald Craufurd Fergusson and the 71st were no strangers to each other. Fergusson had commanded a brigade which took part in the 1805 seizure of the Cape of Good Hope from the Dutch. The Brigade was composed by the 71st, 72nd (Highland) Foot and 93rd (Highland) Foot. The 72nd would later become the 1st Seaforth Highlanders while the 93rd became the 2nd Argyll and Sutherland Highlanders.

[18] This regiment is not identified by the author. Fergusson's brigade consisted of the 36th (Herefordshire) Foot, the 40th Foot and 71st. The records of the 40th state that the regiment did charge the French.

regiment to charge; but, for what cause I could never learn, the whole regiment remained motionless. Colonel Pack, on seeing this, went to the general, and requested permission for us to advance in their stead: and this being granted at once, we, along with the 36th and the 82nd regiments, instantly rushed forward, and fired a tremendous volley, which we saw did great execution. The astonished enemy, on getting such a warm reception, fell into confusion, and began to retrograde; this encouraging us, we gave three hearty cheers, and pressed on: our grenadier company, and the 36th light company with the bayonet, and took six pieces of cannon. We still advanced, and two other pieces of cannon fell into our hands, the enemy not having time to hurry them across a ravine which lay in the way: meanwhile, the enemy continued his retreat, and soon disappeared over an eminence.

A remarkable instance of presentiment of death occurred during the early part of the day. While we were marching to join the rest of the army, one of our men, named Sweeny, an Irishman, happened, somehow or another, to get out of his place in the ranks. An officer observed this, and threatened to punish him for his fault. The spirit of this unhappy man had appeared for some time to be broken, in consequence of frequent reprimands, yet he was never guilty of any heinous crime; he seemed, in short, to have been what is called 'born under an unlucky star', never pleasing his commanders. The last act of power had weighed so heavy on his mind that he was heard to say, 'I will give no more offence': something more was overheard, tending to express the poor fellow's confidence of a speedy dissolution. The words were truly prophetic, for, in less than half an hour afterwards, he was shot dead. I have often heard and read of similar occurrences, but could never account for them: can it be the soul that feels the approach of danger, and warns the grosser senses? Or can it be mere chance? If the latter, how comes it that death is the never-failing consequence, when the men

27

have solemnly assured their incredulous comrades of their internal forebodings? But, after all, I am not so enthusiastic in this belief as to deny that there may have been many who are confident of meeting their death in battle, and yet have escaped safe and sound; but of this kind of persons I never knew one.

Another of our men had his bonnet driven off of his head, and set on fire, by a shell; but he never stopped an instant to reflect on his miraculous escape, for, snatching up the unfortunate Sweeny's bonnet, he clapt it on his head with great *sang froid*, although it (the bonnet) contained some of the blood and brains of its former possessor.

In going over the bloody field, a French general (Brennier) was discovered lying wounded; his horse had been shot under him: his aid-de-camp and an orderly dragoon had

The uniform of the 71st during the First Peninsular Campaign in 1808 is correctly portrayed in this 1817 lithograph. The depiction combines wounded Piper George Clarke piping the regiment into action with the capture of French general Antoine Brennier at the Battle of Vimeiro. *(Reproduced with the permission of the Regimental Trustees of the Royal Highland Fusiliers)*

been endeavouring to extricate him, without effect. They therefore chose to remain faithfully by their master, and were accordingly taken along with him. The appearance of the aid-de-camp was shocking; he had been wounded about the mouth, which occasioned such a flow of blood as to dye his breast and white trowsers quite scarlet. This officer's horse, a beautiful Arabian, was seized as a lawful prize by one of our men; but Colonel Pack deprived him of it, on account of his well-known intemperate habits.

The story of Corporal Mackay capturing General Brennier, and magnanimously refusing his proffered presents, has often been written and spoken of. The real truth of the matter was this: – An Irish lad, named Gaven,[19] was the first that espied the general, and without hesitation he made him prisoner, exclaiming at the same time, 'By Jasus! I have taken the sarjant-major of the French.' Just at that time Mackay came up, and took him out of Gaven's hands; and then it was that the watch and purse were offered, and refused, – Mackay knowing it would be too barefaced a trick to take what should have belonged to another, particularly when there were so many witnesses to the transaction. What was the sequel of this? The *pawky* corporal received a gold medal from the Highland Society and his name was highly lauded in every Gazette; finally, I believe, he received a

---

[19] Writing in the late 1840s another old soldier from the regiment, Corporal Balfour Kermack, also attributed Antoine François Brennier's capture to an Irish recruit. But Kermack did not name the Irish soldier and alleged he was not honoured because M'Kay had to prevent him from taking money from the French general. There was a young red-haired Irish soldier in the regiment called John *Gavin* who enlisted in May 1807. He died at the time of the Walcheren Campaign in 1809. Brennier was imprisoned in England but exchanged for Sir John Abercromby, who had been taken prisoner by the French during a visit to France. Brennier visited the Duke of Wellington before leaving for France and borrowed £500 from him. The debt was never repaid and Brennier fought the British again in Spain.

commission![20] If there is any merit in the thing, poor Gaven should have had it; yet he never received either honour or reward. What was the cause of this injustice, is the natural question? I blush to answer: it was because Mackay was a Scotchman, and, furthermore, a Highlander; the latter was an infallible recommendation to a set of old drivellers, who lay, and still lie, constantly on the watch, to hunt out and blaze forth to the world anything tending to distinguish the Highland name, – sometimes despite the truth.

I am not yet done with this general, or at least with his sword. It is strange, but true, that this sword was destined to occasion both trouble and danger, not only to me, but to the whole of the company to which I belonged. The sword had fallen into the possession of one of the men, who afterwards presented it to our captain, who unfortunately thought it proper to wear it. This did not escape the notice of the colonel, who immediately forbade him from carrying it any longer. Even after this, our worthy colonel had an antipathy to the company, as if we were all to blame in this paltry affair. 'We could do nothing right' after this; and on one occasion the whole company was ordered out to the field, when only twelve men out of each of the other companies was sent. Perhaps some may think that this was an honour, instead of a punishment, to us; but at that disastrous time (the period of the retreat from Corunna), fatigue and misery quelled every idea of glory: – but more of this hereafter.

I return to the principal subject. While several of us were around General Brennier, the French orderly dragoon, who

---

[20] M'Kay was commissioned into the 4th West India Regiment. Contemporary newspaper reports of Brennier's capture attributed it to a Cpl. Ross and it is thought that M'Kay may have joined the 71st under that name. Bugler John Mcfarlane in the notebook he kept relating to his war service recorded only that M'Kay escorted Brennier to the regimental headquarters rather than attributing the general's capture to him.

had remained by him, thought proper to clap spurs to his horse, and set off at full speed. Astonished by this, we stood looking at the rapid flight of our supposed prisoner; but soon recollecting ourselves, a shower of bullets were sent after him, and I believe fully a hundred muskets were discharged without effect. His temerity was successful; he escaped over the hill. After the armistice, I saw this man in our camp, and heard him laughing at his own *ruse de guerre*. While we were resting on our arms, a body of cavalry was suffered to approach us, under the idea that they were Portugueze; but on our discovering them to be French, by their preparations to fall upon us, we made ready to receive them in no friendly manner: on observing this, they thought it proper to make a precipitate retreat. The French and Portugueze cavalry were then so much alike in appearance, that the latter had taken the precaution to tie white strings around their arms, in order to prevent mistakes; but these French had artfully done the same thing.

The day being oppressively hot, we had piled our arms, erroneously concluding that our labours were over, at least for the day. We were accordingly refreshing ourselves by drinking water, and making frequent attacks on the grapes in a vineyard, when the advance of the French a second time was announced by the clang of trumpets and beating of drums, – which latter action, as it appeared, was much easier performed than beating us. We soon caught up our arms, and retired a short distance. By this time the enemy were within ken; but immediately on our giving them another astounding and destructive volley, they put about, and ran up the hill with surprising speed. We ascended the hill in pursuit of them; but on arriving at the top, we found that victory had declared decidedly for the British. Thus ended the battle of Vimiera.

We were much amused while resting from our gory toil, by seeing one of our men taking the remains of a shirt off his back, and then drawing on a dead Frenchman's smock-frock in its stead, – his own shirt, it seems, being in anything but good condition. Sir Arthur Wellesley now came up, and passed some very high encomiums on us: and well he might, for there is little vanity in asserting that the 71st contributed in no small degree to the success of this eventful day; a melancholy proof of this is the fact that we had 119 killed and wounded in our regiment alone.[21]

Some may think that I have not given a general account of the battle of Vimiera; perhaps in this they are right, – but how can a private soldier pretend to see a whole engagement? The thing will plainly be seen to be utterly impossible, when it is considered, that the length of a stone's cast is often the extent of his view, while the conflict sometimes extends over miles. Such being the case, I will confine myself chiefly to what came under my own immediate observation; which I dare say will satisfy the reader better than if I had made up my narrative from gazettes, or stolen from others.

The conclusion of this campaign in Portugal is well known, and displayed an additional proof of the ill effects of allowing British commanders to become cabinet ministers. A foolish armistice was entered into by Wellesley and others,[22] by which the French were allowed to evacuate the country, loaded with the plunder of the Portugueze; but as I had, to use the vulgar expression, as

---

[21] This figure is generally accepted as being reasonably accurate, though one of the regiment's officers wrote to a friend that there were 105 casualties and a newspaper at the time listed 103. Amongst the officers seriously injured was the acting adjutant Robert McAlpin, who was not wounded by the French but fell from a rock he had climbed to get a better view of the fighting.

[22] The infamous Convention of Cintra. Wellesley later claimed to have signed the agreement under protest. His two superiors, Lieutenant General Hew Dalrymple and Lieutenant General Harry Burrard were generally blamed for agreeing to convey the French home, complete with their loot, in British ships.

little to do with the armistice as the man on the moon, I shall pass over it here.

After the battle of Vimiera, we marched to Torres Vedra, and from thence to the banks of the Tagus: here we saw ten Russian men-of-war at anchor. The whole of this delightful march was extremely pleasant, every spot being in the highest state of cultivation, the climate fine, the face of the country beautiful, in short, differing widely, in all respects, from the bleak glens of Scotland. We continued to wend our way along the edge of the majestic Tagus for six or seven miles, till the city of Lisbon rose to our view. This sight was grand beyond description; but we afterwards found that the often-repeated accounts of its filthy interior and beautiful exterior, were perfectly correct, it being exactly similar, in this respect, to what we have heard of Constantinople and other Mediterranean cities. We entered and encamped in the Queen's Park, a large green in the vicinity of Lisbon, the French being at that time quartered in the city. No sooner had we pitched our tents, than immense crowds of citizens came out to see us, all ranks; Colonel Pack, wishing to amuse them, ordered the band to play. I happening to be posted to keep the people from incommoding the musicians, was accosted by a fat priest, in good English, who inquired if there were any Lincolnshire men in our regiment? I was unable to give him any information on this point. I said that there were few Englishmen among us; that we were mostly Scotchmen. He then told me that he was an Englishman himself, – thus accounting for his knowledge of our language. The good-humoured priest on parting offered me some money, which I refused.

Next day new tartan trowsers[23] were served out, our old ones being in a miserably tattered state, owing to the effects

---

[23] All of the lower ranks, with the exception of the regimental pipers, were clothed in tartan trews at this time. The officers usually wore grey or white trousers.

of our campaign. They were now thrown away: this produced a fearful scuffle among some of the lower orders of Portugueze, every one of them contending with the utmost noise and fury, for the possession of a pair of *breeks*. To their honour it must be said, however, or rather to free them, in some degree from national reproach, I must say that when it was discovered that the clothes were filled with myriads of those disgusting insects which are the usual companions of poverty and campaigning, they threw the clothes down with every sign of aversion. Perhaps it is necessary here to apologise or account for our seeming uncleanliness; this is an easy task. Figure to yourself, reader, men landing from a crowded transport without receiving the luxury of clean linen, marching and bivouacking for weeks together without ever putting off their clothes; and your wonder will then cease.

One day a party of our men was sent down to protect the embarkation of some sick and wounded French from the ruthless violence of a Portugueze mob. During the whole of our stay in the park, the city was illuminated every night, on account, I presume, of the expulsion of the Gallic invaders. The ostrich feathers on our Highland bonnets had become so much the admiration of the Portugueze ladies, that no less than a dollar was offered for each of them by the hawkers about the camp; and this induced some of the villains amongst us to rob their comrades. I suffered in this way, in common with some others, having my bonnet completely plucked while I was asleep. Instead of receiving even commiseration for my loss, I was compelled to pay 2*l.* sterling for a new bonnet, and was in danger of being flogged besides: such is military justice!

Several deserters came over here from the French army to the British. They were of different nations, Swiss, Germans and Italians;[24] nearly the whole of them, about

---

[24] It has been suggested by some authors that the large number of non-Frenchmen serving with Napoleon's forces in Portugal and Spain was a factor in the brutality seen during the campaigns.

twenty in number, chose to enlist in our regiment, I know not for what reason, (as every corps in our army was open to them), unless the wearing of tartan was considered as a fine thing by these mercenary fellows. It is a common saying among us, that they could serve three kings with one pair of shoes! One of the Italians was possessed of Herculean strength; he would sometimes carry a log of wood which three of us could scarcely move!

Chapter Two

The month of October had arrived, when we were roused from our repose, by receiving orders to advance into Spain. The beginning of winter was no auspicious time to commence our deplorable march, but of course we could only murmur secretly at the unwelcome news, and prepare to meet the worst.

The 71st were part of Glasgow-born Lieutenant General Sir John Moore's army when it retreated through Spain to Corunna.

Sir John Moore[1] now superseded Wellesley in command of the army, the whole of which was broken up into several divisions, which were to take different routes, but all to rendezvous about Salamanca. Sir John Hope[2] being intrusted with the command of a division, consisting of the 71st, 2nd,[3] 36th, and 92nd regiments, as well as the artillery of the army, we all moved off from Lisbon and marched along the side of the Tagus; we then crossed the river at Abrantes.

I was billeted that night, along with some others, upon an old Portugueze woman. We were, however, in danger of being expelled from her house, through the levity of one of our men. Seeing that the chimney piece was covered with small images of saints, he inquired their names, with an affected air of gravity; the old woman answered his questions with great politeness, until, laying his hands upon one,

---

[1] Sir John Moore, the son of a Glasgow doctor, first saw action during the American Revolution when he served with the 82nd Foot, better known as Hamilton's Regiment and which was disbanded at the end of the conflict. He created the infantry Light Brigade at Shorncliffe in 1803. The 43rd (Monmouthshire) Foot, 51st (2nd Yorkshire West Riding) Foot and 95th (Rifle Corps) Foot were all trained according to Moore's innovative principles. The 5th Battalion of the 60th (Royal American) Foot was also trained in light infantry tactics. Moore's links to the Whig party damaged his prospects of senior command despite a sterling performance during the Egyptian campaign in 1801. It took the disgrace of Wellington, Burrard and Dalrymple after the Convention of Cintra before he was given command of the British troops in Portugal. He was mortally wounded at Corunna. Two of his four division commanders during the campaign were former officers of the 71st: Sir David Baird and Alexander MacKenzie Fraser.

[2] The 71st was part of Catlin Craufurd's brigade. Sir John Hope, the Scots commander of the 2nd Division, took over command of the troops at Corunna after Moore's death and supervised the British evacuation. He was second-in-command of the British troops in the peninsula 1813–14. He was wounded and captured at Bayonne in 1814. Craufurd died of a fever at Arbantes in September 1810.

[3] The 2nd (Queen's Royal) Foot.

38

he told her, that he knew very well this was the figure of the *Diablo*. Horrified at the supposed impiety of the remark, she ran out of the house mumbling imprecations on our heads. We were somewhat alarmed soon after, by an officer entering the place; he had been sent by Colonel Pack to inquire into the matter, – for it seems she had run open-mouthed to complain to him of the 'blasphemous heretics': however, the officer, seeing the thing in its proper light, quietly went away.

Passing through Porto Ligero, we arrived at Campo Mayor, where we lay for a fortnight in the old battery. Bidding adieu to the kingdom of Portugal for a while, we continued our march to Badajoz,[4] a frontier town of Spain. A number of citizens of that place were in waiting for our arrival, and welcomed us with loud acclamations.

After lying ten days in the barracks of Badajoz, we started again, passed through Merida, the capital of Estremadura; from thence we trudged through Truxillo, famous for being the birth-place of Pizarro, the conqueror of Peru; then crossed the Tagus again at Almaraz; passed through Talavera, well known as the scene of a bloody battle between the French and British,[5] not long after this period. Continuing our march, we arrived at the town of Escurial, having, at one time, approached so near to Madrid, that we could plainly distinguish its spires.

In the course of this march we had not the opportunities of knowing the manners and customs of the inhabitants, which we afterwards had; however, we could not but see something of them, even hurried as our journey was. The

---

[4] Badajoz and its fortifications controlled one of the main routes into Spain from Portugal.

[5] The Battle of Talavera was fought in July 1809. After two days of fighting, the British, outnumbered two-to-one and commanded by Wellesley, drove the French off. Casualties were heavy, 7,270 French against 5,370 British, and both sides retreated afterwards.

character of the men was incomprehensible to us, excepting that we saw they considered us as uninvited intruders. As for the women, much could not be said for their virtue. When we entered Spanish towns, we invariably found crowds of the people receiving us with the most hospitable looks, and bawling loudly the kindest wishes for our long life, and so forth. But when our billets were served out, and we had gone to the places designated in them, the doors were always fast, and the 'viva' people nowhere to be seen; and if we chanced to find any of the neighbours, we were told that the inmates of the houses were from home. Finding that they were attempting to 'humbug' us, we henceforth laid down a system which always produced the desired effect. This was, to commence an attack on the billeted doors with the but-ends of our muskets: no sooner had we begun this, than the women of the houses were seen running towards us, holding their keys, to shew that the doors could now be opened. It was in this manner that we at length generally obtained admission.

Warned by experience, our men, instead of receiving the congratulations of the Spaniards at the ends of towns with complacency, only answered them with curses; being well aware, that the loudest of the hollow well-wishers would be the first to become invisible when the night's quarters were in the case. After all, the poor devils could not be blamed, considering that they had been already so harassed and worried by the French armies. It is true that we came as friends; but it is well known, even in our own country, what inconveniences billeted soldiers occasion to a poor family.

When we were once housed, the Spaniards were very liberal in their *offers* of meat, but it was evidently with the expectation of our refusal; their oil and garlic being still detestable to us. Their fire-places were generally hung around with fine sausages, of which, I believe, it would not have required great eloquence to make us accept; but we seldom or never got the offer, I presume for this very reason.

The wary people invariably sat up all night when we were in their houses and watched us, as we lay on the floor, with the eyes of lynxes: they had, indeed, some reason, as several attempts were made to pilfer their sausages; but in this we were seldom successful, a little salt being in general the amount of our thefts. That article hung in a box near the fire-place, exactly similar to what is usual in the common houses of Scotland.

I mentioned our arrival in Escurial before. The town is remarkable for containing a palace of the kings of Spain, which is said to be the largest building in Europe. I went down one day to this place, along with two of our men, and meeting a priest by the way, he politely took us into the palace, and after shewing us part of it, he led us to his own apartment, where we found two other priests. These jovial fellows soon produced some case-bottles of generous wine and plenty of cigars, which the whole of us fell upon with great good will, and we became as friendly as if we had been acquainted with one another for many years. However, it was only one of the three Scotchmen of the party that could talk Spanish well; he had been in South America.[6] Conse-quently the priests and he kept up what, I presume, was a very interesting conversation about that country: but as I and my comrade could understand little or nothing of this, we sat silently quaffing our wine and smoking with 'tranquil delight'. I felt it strange to be sitting in such a friendly manner with Spanish Catholic priests, – men whom I had so often heard represented as a sort of demi-devils; who, no doubt, had in the same way considered us heretics in a similar light. When will religious prejudice completely disappear from the face of the earth, as it did (at least to appearance) in our humble case?

---

[6] The 71st had a higher proportion of Spanish speakers in its ranks than most British regiments, thanks to the time many members spent as prisoners of war in Argentina after the Buenos Aires debacle.

Another day, a party of officers and men having gone to see the palace, I went a second time. On entering, I found the party coming out of the Pantheon, or tombs of the Spanish monarchs. I therefore lost this sight, but was abundantly compensated by seeing the rest of this superb place. Certainly I had no idea that such grandeur existed; one of the numerous halls exceeded any of the rest in this respect; its floor was beautifully chequered with black and white marble; it contained also a magnificent altar, with statues of Christ and the Virgin Mary, of solid gold! There were a number of courts throughout the place, each containing a *jet d'eau*, and a fountain filled with gold fish. The walls of every apartment and lobby were covered with paintings; but being no connoisseur in the arts, I cannot descant upon the respective merits of their painters; all that I will venture to say is, that they pleased me highly. The subjects were chiefly sacred, – views of purgatory, representations of miracles; portraits of apostles, saints, sinners, priests, and devils.

In all parts of the palace figures of gridirons are to be seen; indeed, the building itself is in that form, out of respect to the martyrdom of St. Lawrence, who, it seems, was roasted to death on one of those instruments. This huge monument of bigotry and profusion was built at the expense of 3,300,000 pounds, by Philip the Second, in consequences of the success of his prayer that he might gain a victory over the French. The palace contains a pantheon, a church, and a convent; 4,000 windows and 8,000 doors; 3,000 priests were lodged and fed there when we visited it first, not one remained the next time we entered the country.

But our short dream of pleasure was again disturbed by the issuing of an order to march. This word strongly reminded us that we were not travelling either for instruction or amusement, that we had no will of our own; and, in short, that we were slaves, that must kill or be killed, or starve, or perish with cold, or walk to the end of the world if commanded.

Leaving the Escurial, after a stay of five days, we crossed a pass in a chain of mountains, and continued our march to join the main body of the British army. One night I was billeted with some others, in a house where we were shewn into a miserable dog-hole of an apartment: seeing better rooms in the place, we used the military freedom of removing and taking possession of one of them. This act drew upon us the ire of the inhabitants, and we were assailed with a dreadful storm of oaths and imprecations. One of our men, the best Spanish scholar among us, instantly arose and attacked them in turn with their own weapons, pouring out volleys of the bitterest words he could devise. To our astonishment, this, instead of adding fuel to the flame, produced immediate reconciliation, and the greatest harmony reigned among us during the remainder of our stay.

One of our officers having got possession of a pony, thought proper to mount it while upon the march next day. No doubt it was his intention to ease his aching feet; but being a very unsightly rider, and no favourite in the regiment to boot, we saw our opportunity and embraced it; a shout of derision burst simultaneously from every lip, the noise of which alarmed the pony so much that it went off at full speed. Our hero, apparently, had not calculated upon such a 'show off'; for he exclaimed in tremulous accents, 'Oh what a fall I shall get!' Horror was visibly depicted on his countenance; however, he grasped the saddle firmly, and continued to roar manfully for help; but this no person seemed in a hurry to afford; on the contrary, the whole regiment was convulsed with laughter, to see their arch enemy for once in such a disgraceful situation, – even the officers joined in the laugh. The whole concluded with the unfortunate horseman's overthrow, with, however, very little damage to himself, as he got up, uttering curses, 'not loud, but deep'. For a long time after this he was pretty well humbled by his fall.

Intelligence having arrived of the rapid advance of the French towards Madrid, our division hastened to overtake Moore's army. In our bivouac that night we took great precautions, forming a square about ourselves with the guns, in order to prevent a surprise. Next morning, in passing through a village, the inhabitants brought out several casks of aguadiente[7] to the roadside, and treated every man of us as we marched by. At length we arrived at Alva de Tormas, where it began to be whispered, that the French were pouring into Spain in such numbers that we must be driven out of the country. Hurrying on, we now joined the main body of our army near Salamanca.

We had some diversion on the road with the hypocrisy of two fellows: one of them, it appears, had stolen a hen and deposited it in his haversack; but being unaware that there was a hole in it, the hen's head came out and hung dangling in the sight of every person in his rear. His comrades, with the intention of quizzing him, brought on the subject of pilfering from the Spaniards, and every now and then one would give a pull at the head, till at last almost the whole of the fowl was exposed to view. Meanwhile the man trudged on, totally unconscious of our sport, and joining heartily in uttering the bitterest invectives against those who would rob the poor inhabitants! In due time he was warned of what was behind him; and it may easily be conceived what his looks and sensations were in consequence.

The other fellow's case was something of a similar nature. We all knew that his haversack was filled with stolen sausages, a dog having followed at his heels for a whole day. The same trick was played again; the hypocrite professed also to have a mortal detestation of all plunderers; he was accordingly justly exposed to derision.

About this time it fell to my lot to be appointed one of the commissary's guards (twelve in number); that is to say,

---

[7] Spanish brandy.

44

I had to guard the waggons of provisions and wine. Although this job had the appearance of being good, I found it totally the reverse, having far harder service to perform than if I had been along with the regiment; the lazy waggons being constantly in the rear of a retreating army, and thereby more exposed to the attacks of the enemy's advanced parties. The first night of my being on guard it was so dreadfully cold, that I could not even taste some wine which an artilleryman offered, me: some of my comrades it appears, could drink well enough, however, – for a pigskin of liquor was stolen from the waggons in the course of the night. The commissary was very wroth on discovering his loss; he menaced us with a court martial, of which the slight punishment of hanging was to be the result. We continued crawling along the road at a snail's pace, when we came up on the way with a soldier's wife and three wretched children,[8] who had fallen behind the army; they were accommodated in our waggons. At length we arrived at a village, when it was getting dark. Our commissary,[9] wishing to see the alcalde[10] of the place, alighted, and, tying his horse to a gate, went to look for him.

When the alcalde was found, after a long search, the commissary went to untie his horse, but found that some of the honest villagers had saved him that trouble, there being no trace of the animal to be seen. The enraged commissary,

---

[8] Each regiment was allowed five or six soldiers' wives per company on its ration strength. They acted as laundresses and helped around camp. Moore tried, with little success, to leave 1,200 women and children in Portugal when his army marched into Spain. The author has more to say about wives in the next chapter.

[9] The commissaries were civilians responsible for supplying the regiments with food and clothing. Ensign William Gavin in his diary names the 71st's as Paddy Carey and reports that he was drowned when the boat he was in during the evacuation from Corunna was holed by a French cannon ball. His profits, in the form of gold and silver coin, went to the bottom of the harbour with him.

[10] The mayor or chief magistrate of a Spanish town.

maddened at his repeated losses, began to storm and swear in the most horrible manner; but bethinking himself that this vapouring would not bring back his steed, he made a bold attempt to play off a *ruse de guerre*, a la Captain Cook:[11] – seizing the alcalde, he told him that he was a prisoner until the horse was brought back. But this would not do, – the worthy alcalde laughed him to scorn; so that he had to suffer the misfortune quietly.

No corner being now left in his heart for pity, we were ordered to move on to Sahagun, although it was three leagues distant, and the night pitch dark. A hundred yards had scarcely been gone over, when we were obliged to halt, in consequence of the frost being intense, and the waggon mules unshod. Never shall I forget that dreadful night, through the whole of which I had to stand in the street of this inhospitable village, where no shelter was to be had. I was so benumbed with cold, and oppressed with sleep, that I fell several times to the ground, in spite of my endeavours to remain upright, by leaning on my musket. Meanwhile the muleteers were snug in the waggons: one of them handed out some wine to me, on condition that I was to take charge of two spare mules till the morning. But I had not the beasts long under my surveillance, – for the commissary came up with one of our men and a Spanish guide, and ordered them to take the mules and ride forward to Sahagun, to inform General Moore of the cause of our delay. Not daring to resist this command, I reluctantly surrendered my trust. Daylight at length appeared, and the rays of the sun soon began to melt the frost; this enabled us to move on, and at last we reached Sahagun.

The poor muleteer, on missing his mules, inquired very anxiously of me about them; and on my informing him, as well as I could of the particulars, he shook his head, as

---

[11] The Royal Navy's explorer Captain James Cook, who was famous for bluffing native chieftains during his Pacific voyages.

much as to say, that they were for ever lost. His suspicions were verified; for after the commission had been delivered, the rascally guide, having been intrusted to take back the mules, seized the opportunity of making off with them, never to return.

I now quitted with pleasure the old crusty commissary's service, and joined my regiment. We lay in Sahagun for some days. One evening we were turned out suddenly about six o'clock, and told to have our flints in good order, – but, after all, nothing of moment was done, though we stood till twelve o'clock at night, cooling our heels in the streets, and then marched about a mile out of the town; but the intenseness of the frost still impeded the progress of the artillery so much, that we were forced to return to our old quarters.

We marched on to Benevente. About this time some of our parties had a skirmish with the French, and several prisoners were brought in, among whom was General Lefebvre.[12] We continued our disastrous retreat, for it could now only be so called; the French pursuing us sharply, in mighty numbers. The roads began now to be in a terrible state, in consequence of a continual rain; the mud rose as high as our knees; and this destroyed all appearance of order in the march, every one trying to pick his way in the best manner he could. As far as the eye could reach, our army had the resemblance of a straggling flock of drenched ducks, rather than of bold warriors. Wading like the rest, very dolefully along, I stept upon a seemingly smooth and dry part of the road; and before I knew where I was, I found myself up to the middle in mud. The mud was so tough, that, in spite of every effort to extricate myself, I stuck fast for a

---

[12] Marshal François Lefebvre. He rose from the rank of private in the royal guard and was captured by the 11th Hussars in Spain in 1808. He broke his parole while a prisoner in Cheltenham in 1812 and rejoined the French army.

considerable time, during which no endeavours were made to assist me, every one being too busily engaged with his own misfortunes to mind those of others.

Having succeeded, at length, in getting out of the slough, although at the expense of a pair of shoes, I made shift to get up to the regiment. Arriving at a village, we obtained quarters. Being much in want of a pair of good shoes, a thought came into my head (God forgive me) of possessing myself of a stout pair, belonging to my Spanish landlord. They lay very temptingly in view; but considering that if I was to cram them at once into my haversack, they might be missed before I could get out of the house, and being un-willing to abide the disagreeable consequences of this, I hit upon a seemingly better scheme, of covering them, as it were by chance, with my knapsack and accoutrements. I lay till morning in full expectation of possessing the prize but my plan was completely defeated by the old Spaniard's rising early, and commencing a search for his brogues. I lay still knowing well what he was looking for, hugging myself with the idea that the scheme was so laid, that if they were discovered no blame could be attached to any one, At length the old don, in turning over every thing, perceived the identical shoes, and 'grinning horribly a ghastly smile', – he lugged them triumphantly forth, and went away without saying any thing.

Next morning, continuing our *wade*, we arrived at a river, and forded it. An officer, before crossing, ordered one of the men to carry him over; but just as he had mounted the man's back, Colonel Pack observed the transaction, and immediately ordered the delicate gentleman to be set down, and to ford the water himself. After passing through the towns of Astorga and Villa Franca, we began the ascent of an exceedingly high mountain, on the first day of the year 1809. The want of provisions was now seriously felt; and this, united to the fatigue, caused many to fall, never to rise again.

In ransacking a village which we came to, some potatoes and honey were found: this allayed the pain of our gnawing stomachs a little: scarcely any of us slept during the whole night, the cooking of the potatoes engrossing almost all our attention. We then marched to the town of Lugo, where we remained one night and part of a day; but the enemy being just at our heels, it was not thought prudent to stay longer; we were therefore obliged to evacuate the town, and bivouac on its outside, with heavy hearts. It was, indeed, a miserable night: thrust out to the storm, and the rain lashing on me in torrents, I threw myself down in the mud, on the lee side of a stone dyke, as the best shelter I could find. Certainly there was no respect of persons here: the elements are remarkably impartial in such cases as these; and on looking round the field I saw Colonel Pack squatting close by my side.

The French had been long hanging on our rear like a cloud, which now, however, seemed as if it were about to burst, – as on the morning of the next day they attacked us in earnest. Twelve men out of each of the other companies, and the whole of ours, were sent out to stem their way. I was among the party that was placed as a reserve: in this situation the enemy began peppering us with cannon-balls, upon which we had recourse to our old system of sitting down. Happening to be under a tree, it was struck several times, and the man who sat next me got his musket broke to splinters in his hand, without receiving the slightest injury; the same ball, after forcing its way through a stone wall, continued its course to the very lines. Darkness put an end to the skirmish, in which an odd incident had occurred. One of the men actually brought in a French prisoner *hooked by the cheek with his fixed bayonet*. To prevent mistakes, it is necessary to mention, that this was not done with any cruel intention, but in the mere hurry of the moment.

Grim hunger was again preying on our vitals, without any prospect of our driving him out; when one of our company fortunately got hold of a bullock, which it appears had made

49

its escape from the French. The poor animal apparently did not better its condition by desertion, as the time was but short before it was a bleeding corpse. The generous captor shared the prize with his comrades in the most honourable manner; and shortly after he received a humble message from Colonel Pack, begging a present of the heart, which request was not only complied with, but the kidneys were given in addition. This was not the only instance of officers being obliged to solicit a meal from privates: just at this very time several of them came and begged a few potatoes from us. Those officers who were well liked received a supply with the greatest alacrity on our part, while the tyrannical ones were served with a grudge.

Some of our men having been sent down to a farm-house for straw, met there with a number of French soldiers on the same errand.[13] Reciprocal civilities passed between them, giving the direct lie to any national antipathy. In the course of the night we were roused by orders to fall in – no words were to be spoken, or pipes lighted. When we had marched on a short way, one of the men was seized with a violent cramp in the stomach, which set him a roaring like a bull: this noise being contrary to orders, we were forced to answer the poor fellow's cries with blows, to keep him quiet, no other method having any effect. It was still quite dark, when we marched through the town of Lugo. About this time, several pieces of cannon were buried,[14] and their carriages burned, to prevent the enemy from reaping any benefit by them.

In the middle of the day we halted in a turnip field. Even that miserable vegetable was considered delicious food; and the whole regiment attacked them as eagerly as famished

---

[13] Memoirs from the Peninsular War abound with tales of friendly relations between British and French troops when not engaged in battle. One story has it that a British officer once found one of his sentries carrying two muskets; his own and that of a French sentry who had gone to fetch some brandy.

[14] A total of six cannon were buried.

wolves would have done a dead horse: for my part, never having been able to eat these roots, I was obliged to hush my hunger to sleep; although this, it may be easily conceived, was somewhat difficult. A constant pitiless rain continued to fall. A party of us having been sent to a farmhouse for straw to litter ourselves in our muddy beds for the night, we received intelligence that apples were discovered up in the loft. This was, indeed, joyful news; hunger lending speed to my heels, I ran with inconceivable velocity to the place; but, alas! every apple had been already bagged, by crowds from every regiment in the army. Bearing up under this misfortune with as much equanimity as possible, I fortunately chanced to enter an unfrequented room in the house, and there discovered a quantity of flour. Without waiting to feast my eyes long on the glorious sight, I was proceeding to unloose my haversack, when I found myself so benumbed with cold, that I was actually obliged to cut it from my side. Filling our haversacks to the mouth, and taking wisps of straw under our arms, as a kind of excuse, we 'went on our way rejoicing', leaving crowds who had scented the precious grain busily engaged in sweeping it into their sacks. Our starving comrades were highly delighted to see us return with such a valuable commodity, instead of worthless straw.

Some hog's-lard being produced, fires were lighted on every side; and some of our most experienced bakers soon made up a quantity of flour cakes, with which we gorged ourselves to our hearts' content. I never tasted a sweeter meal in all my life than this. Although the rain continued with unabated violence, I lay down in the cold mud, and slept as sound as if I had been in the best bed: such are the wonderful effects of a good bellyful after long abstinence: and this proves also, that amidst the most abject misery, there is such a thing as pleasure. Some overplus[15] cakes

---

[15] Archaic word for surplus.

belonging to me were put into my comrade's haversack, my own being too wet.

We again marched on; but scarcely had I walked an hour when I lost my shoes, and was obliged to trudge on barefooted. Many of the officers were in the same state; some of them attempted to defend their feet by wrapping pieces of blanket round them. My sufferings were now dreadful. Every thing in the shape of stockings being long since gone, the constant friction of the wet trowsers rubbed the skin completely off my legs, and the raw fleshy feeling as if cauterised, increased my torments to an indescribable degree. But many were in a far worse condition, and lay down completely exhausted with excess of fatigue and misery, waiting impatiently for death to relieve their pangs. The regiments in the immediate rear were, comparatively speaking, in greater distress than ourselves having, in addition to all our sufferings, the enemy's cavalry to contend with.

Order in the march was now totally disregarded, every regiment in the army being intermixed, on account of the best walkers pressing on, and keeping as near the van as possible; while the weaker ones either fell behind or fell for ever. Many fell sound asleep while walking, and then stood in the midst of the road like pillars: no attempts were made to awake them, the cry of 'Keep off' was raised, and every one studiously avoided jostling the sleepers. Three successive times did I fall into this strange condition, in spite of myself.

About this time I saw a dragoon[16] sprawling in the mud, quite drunk, and seemingly unconscious of his miserable situation, laughing and yelling out his bacchanalian

---

[16] When Sergeant John Graham of the 71st attempted to stop a soldier from the 18th Dragoons looting a priest's house, the cavalryman drew his pistol and fired at him. The dragoon was quickly overpowered and arrested. Graham was the regimental paymaster's clerk in 1800 but was promoted to adjutant, with the rank of ensign, in 1809. He was killed as a lieutenant at Fuentes de Onoro in 1811.

ribaldry. This poor wretch undoubtedly became food for the crows in a few short hours. Our cavalry and artillery horses died in such numbers, that nearly the whole road between Lugo and Corunna was strewed with their bloated carcasses.

I daily felt more and more the inconvenience of walking with naked feet; and having cut my toe against a stone, I suffered such excruciating pains, that following the example of others, I threw myself on the ground with a fierce indifference to my fate; death had no longer any terrors for me. While lying in this unenviable condition, I saw General Ferguson, with a number of field-officers and aid-de-camps, riding about, entreating all who lay on the ground to get up, as Corunna was near at hand, and, as an additional entice-ment to get on, the officers cut off a number of knapsacks from the backs of the men. The general came up to two men who lay close by me, and persuaded them to rise, and crawl on: coming to me next, he attempted to encourage me with hopes of a speedy arrival at the ships, and so on; but I told him in firm, but respectful, terms that 'I felt myself unable even to move'. I passed a whole night in this condition, bitterly regretting the want of the cakes which had been put in my comrade's haversack. Perhaps some readers may think me a very unsentimental fellow, if I felt only this animal regret at such a time; but they may set their minds at rest when I assure them that home and friends occupied some of my thoughts.

Daylight coming in, the desire of life returned, and a ray of hope darted into my soul; I made a strenuous effort to rise, and succeeded, though I felt as weak as a child. Leaving many on the ground, never to tell the tale again, I staggered on towards a farm-house which I saw at a distance; and meeting with a pool of water by the way, I walked into it, not with the intention of drowning myself, but of cooling my aching feet and washing my trowsers. After clawing off a quantity of mud and slime, I arrived at the farm-house. Here, if I had not been extremely hungry, a whole train of reflections would have burst in upon me, the house being literally gutted – not a soul was to be seen. Here was a strong proof of the baneful effects of war; or, in other words, the cruelty of man to man.

Having prowled through every room in the house, without finding any thing in the shape of food, I went into the desolate yard, where I spied some bee-hives in a corner, which, it appears, had escaped the notice of the last plunderers, whoever they were. There being no other means of coming at the honey, I knocked down one of the hives with the but-end of my musket, – for which act it seemed I was likely to pay dear; some of the bees sallied out and stung my feet; perhaps the coldness of the wintry weather prevented the rest from attacking me. I filled my haversack with honey, and, after eating as much of it as I could, proceeded on my route. I soon found that this new sort of food did not agree with me after long abstinence; a sudden sickness came over me, and compelled me to lie down on the road, where I fell asleep. I was awakened from my nap by three of the band who were passing by. One of them, who carried a large loaf, seeing that I had honey, offered to exchange a piece of the loaf for some of it; of course I eagerly agreed to this, but found after all, that I could not swallow a morsel of the bread, my weakened jaws refusing to do their duty.

I contrived to hold on my tottering steps for a short distance, and saw by the way four men, of a certain *'gallant'* Scotch regiment,[17] robbing a poor Spanish woman of some bread, –although she was protesting, in the most piteous manner, that she had nothing else to give her starving children. Had not my debilitated state, and the number of my antagonists, prevented me, I would have certainly done every thing in my power to prevent such cruelty and

---

[17] The other Scottish regiments involved in the retreat were the Black Watch, the Cameron Highlanders, the Argyllshire Highlanders, the Royal Scots, the Cameronians and the Gordon Highlanders.

injustice: but some little extenuation may be found in the absolute necessity of the case.

I arrived at the town of Batanzas in a very helpless condition. Colonel Pack was looking out of a window when I entered, apparently watching for the arrival of the stragglers of his own regiment. Seeing me, he asked what was the number of my company; and on my reply, pointed out the house destined for its reception. I entered with full expectation of being the last that would ever arrive of the whole company, which once consisted of eighty men; but now, to my astonishment, nine only out of that number stood before me.[18] We now had three days' allowance of beef and bread served out; and it was the first expense we had occasioned to our country for a long while. We were all in

Lieutenant Colonel Denis Pack commanded the 71st in South Africa, South America, the First Peninsular Campaign and Walcheren. He was later seconded to the Portuguese army and commanded a brigade at the Battle of Waterloo in 1815. After his death in 1823, his widow Elizabeth married Thomas Reynell, who commanded the 71st at Waterloo.

[18] The 71st lost somewhere between ninety-three and ninety-eight men between 19th December and their arrival in Portsmouth following the evacuation from Corunna. The total British losses during Moore's campaign were somewhere between 6,000 and 7,000 men. Gavin records in his diary that of the 2,500 men of Craufurd's brigade who took part in the retreat, fewer than 150 were still marching in formed units by the time they reached the Corunna area. And even they were ragged and shoeless, many without weapons.

such an exhausted state, that even the operation of cooking the provisions was with difficulty accomplished; and this will serve to account for our being highly provoked on discovering that, during the momentary absence of the cook, who was looking for a knife, the whole of our dinner had been carried off by some heartless villains, thus obliging us to renew our toil in preparing a new mess.

By this time, having got new shoes, some shelter and repose, we started again, somewhat refreshed. We had not gone far, till the sea and Corunna burst on our sight. To describe our feelings at this time would be a waste of words; it is, perhaps, rather musty to compare them to those of the ten thousand Greeks;[19] but, as far as I can judge, the comparison would be a just one. Our joy was, however, a little damped on seeing no ships in readiness; without these we were as badly or rather worse off than ever. We took up our quarters in a rope-walk on the outskirts of the town of Corunna.

The next morning we marched out, and encamped by the side of a small rivulet, in order to prevent the enemy from advancing, the stream being fordable at low water. The French had also encamped on the opposite side of the same stream. We lay inactive till next morning, when we were rather alarmed by the blowing up of a powder magazine, about two miles distant: the concussion was so powerful that the ground shook violently under our feet, and the piled arms were levelled with the ground.[20]

---

[19] A reference to the force of 10,000 Greek mercenaries who fought and looted their way 1,000 miles across the Persian Empire to safety around 400 BC after the death of their employer left them stranded in hostile territory. Moore's men retreated around 250 miles.

[20] The destruction of a gunpowder store was ordered to prevent it falling into the hand of the French. It is not clear whether the artillerymen who blew up the store containing 1,500 barrels realised it was next to another store of 4,000 barrels. Witnesses reported two explosions. Several people were killed by falling debris and every window in Corunna was reportedly broken.

On the following day, the 16th of January, 1809, the battle of Corunna took place; but it so happened that we had little to do with the engagement, only four of our companies being engaged, and those but partially.[21] Towards the close of the day, we were ordered to relieve some of the regiments which had suffered most; in marching across a road to effect this, we saw Sir John Moore carried by wounded. The coming on of night put an end to the action, – so that we had to retrace our steps to our old position, having fortunately suffered only the loss of one man killed, an officer and some others wounded.

The history of shooting the cavalry horses is well known,[22] but I confine myself to our own transactions. We bivouacked on the night of the battle, after kindling numerous fires. The ships having arrived, we rose silently in the dead of the night, and leaving some men to keep up the fires, in order to deceive the enemy, we marched off, *'wi little din'* through the town of Corunna, and from thence to the sea side. It was a dark and stormy night; numerous small boats lay pitching and rolling on the troubled waters; and our only light came from the flambeaux held by some naval officers. The scene of confusion that took place baffles all description; nearly the whole of our army was assembled here, in the most tumultuous manner, and every one rushed indiscriminately into the boats, reckless of danger. All control and order were now lost, every one shifting for himself, without regarding the order to keep by his own particular regiment: as usual in such cases *we* followed the example, and were soon scattered among the crowd. The confusion was much

---

[21] The 71st skirmished with the French on 15 January and lost several men killed and wounded. They were stationed on the left of the British position next day and saw little action during the Battle of Corunna.

[22] Only around 250 horses were considered worth evacuating with the army. The rest of the horses were slaughtered. The exact number shot and stabbed is not known but could well have been in excess of 1,000.

increased by the turning loose of the baggage mules as soon as they were unloaded.

Having, with infinite difficulty, forced my way into a crowded boat, we pulled off from the shore. Already many of the men were asleep at the bottom of the boat – such had been their excessive fatigue. The sailors who rowed us, anxious to get rid of their laborious work; put us on board the vessel nearest to the shore, and the consequence of this was, that the vessels which lay farthest out were not half so much incommoded by numbers as our ship was.

Daylight coming on, the French opened a heavy fire of shot and shells upon the transports, from some batteries on the heights; and this unexpected salute terrified the transport captains so much, that several of them gave orders to cut their cables, without first taking the necessary precaution to brace their yards. Five vessels, in consequence of this, ran ashore in the greatest disorder. The foolish master of our vessel, seized with the same consternation (a shell having burst at the stern, filling the whole ship with smoke), was hastening to follow the rash example the others had set, in cutting the cable, when we thought proper to prevent him. An officer of the 38th regiment,[23] who seemed to have some nautical skill, then took the command, ordering the sails to be all set first, and afterwards that the cable should be cut. Although the balls were whizzing through the rigging now and then, the officer's orders were obeyed with great promptitude and coolness, and we were soon running out to sea in fine style; not, however, without having the satisfaction of seeing a British seventy-four come in, and silence with a single broadside the battery which had annoyed us so much.

---

[23] The 38th (1st Staffordshire) Foot.

Chapter Three

Our campaign in the Peninsula had thus ended ingloriously, after a prosperous outset. Such had been exactly the case with the British about a century before. They attempted, under the command of the Earls of Peterborough and Galway, to place Charles the Third on the throne of Spain, in opposition to the wishes of the French and part of the people. Success at first attended them; but the battle of Almanza compelled them to relinquish all hopes of effecting their design, being obliged to evacuate the country entirely. Till the period of which I speak, this had been the only attempt made by Britain to control Spain, with the exception of some predatory naval attacks. Our own case was, as I have already remarked, similar to that to which I have alluded, – it was an attempt to place Ferdinand on the throne in this instance, as in the former, Charles.

It is not difficult to account for our failure; the numerical superiority, of Buonaparte's army to that of ours, together with the apathy: both of Spaniards and Portugueze to the cause, and other circumstances which I may mention; such as making a winter campaign, by order of our government. If our route be traced on a map, it will be seen, that after leaving Portugal, we passed through the provinces of

Estremadura, New Castile, Old Castile, Leon, and Galicia, between the months of October and January. As we advanced northwards from Estremadura, the country became more and more mountainous, till our arrival at Corunna. The year, as it advanced, brought upon us all the horrors of a severe winter. It was never calculated upon, that the climate of the mountainous parts of Spain was so severe. If, on the contrary, we had remained in the fertile plains of Estremadura, or marched southwards, we should never have felt what we did in this respect, as an eternal spring reigns throughout these districts. A close pursuit for hundreds of miles, without a regular supply of provisions; the ragged state of our clothing; our constant exposure to the damp of the ground; bad shoes;[1] and innumerable other inconveniences – all combined, made 6,000 brave fellows bite the dust, or rather the mud. In consequence of this, we were constrained to leave the neighbourhood of this spot, which had been the grave of so many men.

I believe the cause of many deaths, and incalculable sufferings to those who survived their miseries, was owing *solely* to the bad shoes which were furnished to the army by contractors: it was thought a good shoe that would last a week; but the far greater part of them was destroyed in a day or two! Of course, a constant supply could not be kept up at that rate. Many a soldier, poor as he was, would have paid a guinea out of his own pocket cheerfully to get a pair of good shoes.

I must speak here also of the very reprehensible custom of allowing soldiers' wives to follow the army: so far from their being of any service, they were, on the contrary, a constant burden. Washing, which appears naturally a work of theirs, was entirely left to ourselves, not a stitch being ever touched

---

[1] The shoes issued were poor quality. A layer of clay between the soles disintegrated when it became damp and the shoes fell to pieces very quickly.

by them. Their profligate lives were not only the detestation of their own husbands, but even of many other soldiers, – strange as it may appear in the latter instance.

But to return to my narrative: we were leaving the Iberian shores – 'nothing loath'; but we found, to our great inconvenience, that there were 510 of us to be packed on board a very small brig, and the whole of this number had entered the vessel in such disorder, that the amalgamation of our army appeared complete – we having no less than part of seventeen regiments on board. It was found necessary, on account of the crowded state of the ship, to cook at separate times; and, notwithstanding this, it was extremely difficult to find victuals withal; everyone was stealing from another; and serious battles often took place about the privilege of scraping the fragments of burgoo[2] from the sides of the coppers. It being impossible to stir without trampling on the body of someone or other, the hold continually resounded with the oaths and curses of the individuals trampled on; there was even a man smothered in the course of the voyage, but I believe he was intoxicated at the time. We derived some amusement from an officer who was seldom or never absent from the side of the capstan; during the whole voyage, he was continually rubbing his back against it, having long since given up, as a hopeless case, the idea of freeing himself from the innumerable hordes of vermin by which we were infested. As all of us bore the same torments, but with rather more equanimity than this gentleman, some jokes were played off on him from different quarters.

To our unspeakable joy, we arrived safe at Portsmouth; but cruel fortune seemed not yet tired of castigating us, – a sudden gale coming on, compelled us to cut the cable, and allow the vessel to drive on the sands: happily it abated without doing any serious injury. Some sailors were sent to

---

[2] Burgoo was a form of porridge favoured by the Royal Navy.

get us off; this, however, it required several tides to effect. These rude sons of Neptune were always coming and going to and from the vessel, and as they often looked down the hold, they cracked many jokes upon our evident misery.

All the men belonging to the other regiments having been taken ashore left us abundant room. We were soon floated into deep water, and the rest of the regiment now joined us; but still we were all detained on board, – I never could learn for what reason, the rest of the army having been already landed.

Among the women who were put ashore on our arrival at Portsmouth, there was one belonging to our regiment who had rather the appearance of a bundle of rags than of a human being. Upon some of the men calling out to her not to expose the regiment by telling the good English people that such a scare-crow belonged to it, she answered that she would soon have more prize-money than any of us. This eventually turned out true; not long afterwards she joined us again, finely dressed, and having 30*l.* in her pocket. She had procured all this by begging; her lamentable story had taken well, but, I dare say, she got the money more readily on account of having a beautiful child in her arms.

Being all transferred to a different vessel, we were ordered round to Ramsgate, in order to disembark. In passing Beachyhead we got a sudden alarm by the vessel heeling so much that her yards were in the water. A sergeant and twelve men were thrown from their berths to the bottom of the hold; the guns, coppers, and other moveable articles broke loose; and a general cry was raised that we were going down. The danger did not prevent some would-be-wits from saying that there was a 'sergeant's command away to the hold'. In the course of this short voyage I got my only shirt stolen off the rigging while it was drying; but my rage was soothed by new shirts and trowsers being served out to every man of us. Having landed at Ramsgate, we marched to Ashford barracks. Here the old tyrant Death again visited us, and the 91st regiment[3] in particular, with a heavy hand – three or four men dying every day for some time in consequence of brain fever: this was universally allowed to arise from their former fatigues.

We now marched to Braeburnlees, and received a draft of 350 recruits, from Scotland,[4] besides a number of men volunteered into our corps from some English and Irish militia regiments. These reinforcements made us 1,100 strong, and we formed as beautiful a regiment[5] as I ever saw; very different in appearance from what we were on our arrival from Spain. In June 1809 we marched to Portsmouth, and encamped there, while the rest of the army was assembling for the invasion of Walcheren.

The fatal expedition to Walcheren[6] had now been determined upon. We accordingly embarked in the *Belleisle*,[7] a 74-gun ship, having, in addition to our men, some horses and

---

[3] The 91st (Argyllshire Highlanders) Foot. The regiment was deprived of its Highland status in 1809.

[4] From the Glasgow-based 2nd Battalion of the 71st.

[5] In March 1809 the 71st was designated a light infantry unit and ordered to adopt the drills and equipment of the other light infantry regiments – the 43rd, 52nd (Oxfordshire), 68th (Durham) and 85th (Bucks Volunteers). The 71st successfully lobbied to be allowed to retain its kilted pipers and 'Scotch' bonnets with a distinctive red and white diced band around the base. The regiment now became the Highland Light Infantry.

[6] The Dutch were allied to the French at this time and the island of Walcheren was regarded as the key to the Scheldt Estuary and to blocking access to the important port of Antwerp. The British assigned 40,000 troops to the expedition. The Highland Light Infantry were to return to Walcheren in 1944 when, as part of the 52nd Lowland Division, they helped clear the island of Germans. The division's 157th Brigade was made up of the 5th and 6th HLI and the 1st Glasgow Highlanders.

[7] HMS *Belleisle* was a French-built warship captured by the British in 1795 and was part of Admiral Horatio Nelson's fleet at Trafalgar. She was broken up in 1814. A second *Belleisle* was launched in 1819 and in 1847 brought the 71st home from a posting in the West Indies.

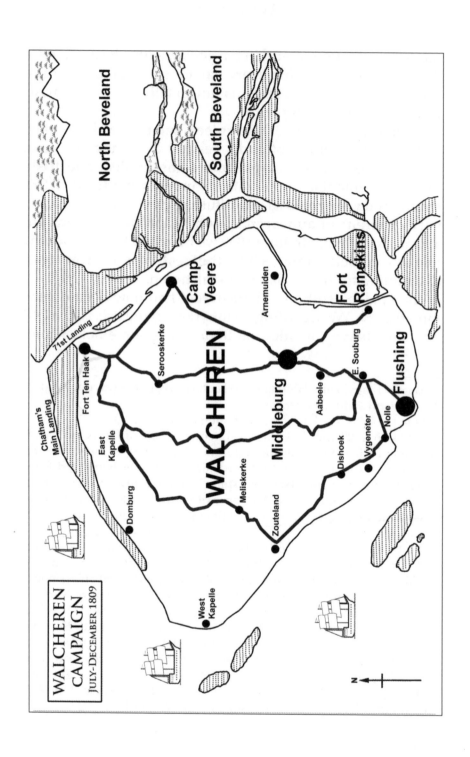

WALCHEREN
CAMPAIGN
JULY–DECEMBER 1809

North Beveland

South Beveland

Chatham's
Main Landing

71st Landing

Fort Ten Haak

East
Kapelle

Domburg

West
Kapelle

Zouteland

Meliskerke

Serooskerke

WALCHEREN

Camp
Veere

Arnemuiden

Middleburg

Aabeele

E. Souburg

Fort
Ramekins

Dishoek

Vygeneter

Nolle

Flushing

N

artillery on board. Having proceeded to Deal, we sailed from that place at three o'clock in the morning, on the 28th of July, 1809. Never will I forget the glorious sight of the most powerful and numerous fleet which ever left the British shores, – the sea looked as if it groaned under the weight of so many vessels, and as far as the eye could reach a wilderness of masts was seen. Thirty-five sail of the line, twenty-three frigates, 179 transports, and an innumerable quantity of small craft composed this mighty armament, containing 39,000 troops, under the command of the Earl of Chatham.[8]

What wonderful revolutions does time make! Scarcely nineteen centuries ago, Caesar invaded Britain with a numerous fleet, and found the inhabitants immersed in the grossest barbarism, and utterly ignorant of sea affairs. Little did he think, I dare say, that the descendants of these very islanders would send forth ships to subdue countries in every quarter of the globe, and reign everywhere undisputed masters of the sea; still less did he think that one of their smallest frigates would have been sufficient to put the whole of his 800 sail to flight.

But to return from this digression: thirteen hours' sailing enabled us to drop our anchors off the island of Walcheren, at four o'clock in the afternoon. Next day, the whole army got into the boats, which all started at a signal for the shore; the landing was successfully performed, one battery only having attempted to annoy us, and that without effect. Seeing some of the enemy lurking in a wood, two of our companies rushed forward, took two pieces of cannon, and some prisoners. We marched towards Campveer;[9] some of

---

[8] The Earl of Chatham was the eldest son of British Prime Minister William Pitt, known as Pitt the Elder. His younger brother William, was also prime minister and was known as Pitt the Younger. The Walcheren Campaign was his only senior command.

[9] Campveer was a fort and town also known as Terr Veere or Camp Veere.

our men entered a fort by the way, which the enemy had evacuated on our approach, and found a good dinner which the French had left, ready cooked. It was quite dark when we arrived at the town of Campveer; but though we trod as lightly as possible, the French sentinel discovered and challenged us. Immediately after this a tremendous fire of grape-shot was opened upon us; but as the garrison fired merely at random, on account of the darkness, we did not suffer so much as if it had been otherwise. However, the scene was appalling enough; there was a constant roar of the guns, the bullets were whizzing audibly, and were crushing or lopping off the branches of the surrounding trees. While in this situation, I was suddenly struck to the ground by a ball which had entered the side of my knapsack; fortunately I escaped unhurt. Finding that we were exposing ourselves needlessly to danger, we retreated, with a loss of sixty killed and wounded;[10] a heavy price indeed, since there had been nothing accomplished. We were obliged to lie all night on the bank of a muddy ditch, with the rain lashing on us the whole time. Being very thirsty, after our midnight wanderings, we were fain to content ourselves with drinking the disgusting and putrid ditch-water. On examining my knapsack, I found the ball had gone through a pair of shoes, broken a soap-box and button-stick to pieces, and finally lodged in a shirt, after passing through eleven folds of it. I kept this ball for some time, but at last threw it away, it being a quarter of a pound in weight and too heavy to carry.

Next day we marched round the town, I presume the intention was to discover its most assailable point. Several shot and shells were thrown at us in doing this, but without doing us any damage. Our guns were hauled by a number

[10] The regiment reported only eighteen killed and wounded. But Gavin's diary put the number of dead at twenty-seven and the wounded at fifty-one. *The Highland Light Infantry* by L. B. Oatts (Leo Cooper, 1968) put the total loss at thirty killed and wounded.

of sailors from the fleet; these fellows being utterly ignorant of land operations, were continually using their sea terms in dragging; such as starboard, and larboard, and so forth. We had some difficulty in keeping them to their work; on one occasion, the whole body disappeared, nobody knew whither, till some Dutchmen came up and informed us, with great agitation, that the tars had forced their way into the houses, and were making some rude attacks on the *frows*. Upon receiving this intelligence, we went forward, and drove them back to the guns at the point of the bayonet.

Finding that nothing could be done in the way of entering the strong town of Campveer, we continued our march to a small village in its environs, and saw on the way a French frigate on fire. She had been endeavouring to escape up the Scheldt, but having grounded in the attempt, the crew had set fire to her: as usual, every gun went off as the flames came to it.

We encamped that night in a hay-field, and a party of us was sent for water; however, not a drop was to be had, except that of the ditches; this miserable island being totally destitute of springs. One of the men seeing a jar in an empty boat, stept on board with the idea of its containing gin, – he raised it to his head, and actually swallowed some of the liquid before he discovered that it was rank train oil.[11] We got plenty of cheap gin in the village; there was as much given for a sixpence as for a shilling — the honest Hollanders not seeming to have the smallest idea of the respective value of English money. Some sharpers among us, seeing the poor people's ignorance in this respect, furbished up their own copper coins, and covering them with quicksilver, passed them off for English coin with great ease; nay, sometimes by merely knocking the eye off a button, and flattening it, the workman obtain the value of a

---

[11] Whale oil.

shilling. I cannot help laughing, to think of an old woman, who kept a kind of grocery shop, giving copper coins to our men in change, and in a few hours afterwards taking them back as sixpences!

Leaving our encampment, we marched on, passing through the town of Middleburg in the night-time; and still continuing our march, we came unawares, in the dusk of the morning, under the guns of Fort Ramekins. Our first warning was given by the enemy's fire, but we made a precipitate retreat, without suffering loss. Having arrived within a short distance of Flushing, we lay there till the rest of the army came up.

Vigorous preparations were now made to bombard the town of Flushing, and our constant employment was, for some time, building a battery. The French, as a last resource, cut the sea dike, with the hope of cramping the operations of the British forces: this was obviated, however, by placing sticks at intervals along the edges of the paths, in the vicinity of Flushing; this precaution enabled us to guide our steps with safety when the full tide inundated the island. A battery, which the enemy had raised near ours, annoyed us exceedingly; we could not march out to relieve our picket, without a fire being opened upon the men. It was therefore resolved upon to attempt the surprisal of this grievous plague. One dark night, two parties were formed; one of them was ordered to advance silently, and storm the battery; the other to follow in the rear, and fill up the cut in the dike if necessary. Everything succeeded as well as could be wished; the first party met with no obstruction till they stumbled over a French drummer: this poor fellow was preparing to beat an alarm, when that trouble was saved him by his being thrown over into the sea, drum and all. Nothing powerful enough presented itself to stop the party's progress; they pressed on, bore down all opposition, took the battery, spiked the guns, secured some prisoners, and returned with a loss of thirty-eight killed and wounded.

Meanwhile our sanguinary bombarding was going on both from land and sea; the ear was stunned with the continual roar of the artillery and the hissing of the rockets;[12] and the heart bled at the sufferings of the devoted Flushing people. Night, the usual time of suspending hostilities, gave no respite: the darkness was dispelled by the burning of the houses, set on fire by the shells; of these articles I have counted fourteen in the air at one time – such was the immense number thrown. By day the line-of-battle ships ranged close to the town, and poured in their tremendous broadsides, then, wheeling round, the dose was repeated from the other sides; I could discern distinctly the dreadful effects of each broadside, an immense cloud of dust marking the place, where perhaps a stately building stood the moment before! The resistance offered to us was, comparatively speaking, feeble; and it appeared afterwards that the wily Frenchmen had compelled the unfortunate citizens to work the guns against us, and, by keeping aloof, saved their own bacon; the chief loss thus fell upon the Hollanders, both in lives and effects. Four days of incessant battering having reduced Flushing to a heap of smoking ruins, the French, finding that their situation was no longer tenable, surrendered at discretion.[13] Having seen the garrison march out prisoners of war, we proceeded to Middleburg.

About this time, that fatal sickness which conducted so many to their last home, made its appearance: the medical men were as yet unaware of what the complaint was, or

---

[12] This was the third occasion on which the British used the rockets developed by Colonel William Congreve. The Royal Navy had first used them in October 1806 in an attack on Boulogne. The 71st reputedly furnished men for a rocket battery which fought at the Battle of Leipzig in 1813.

[13] The French garrison included the Legion Irlandaise, which was made up of Irish deserters, former prisoners of war and admirers of Napoleon.

what it arose from; they knew not that it was the ague, that scourge of marshy countries. Continuing our march, we arrived once more at Campveer, the place being now in our possession. Here we found the troops in a deplorable state; disease and death were reigning triumphant. The 84th regiment,[14] which we were appointed to relieve, was already seized with the disease[15] – the men were nearly all sick or dead; the 68th and 85th were in the same predicament shortly afterwards, their shattered remains were therefore sent off to England, by which means we were left alone in the town.

It was soon found that we were not to pass the ordeal of Campveer ague with impunity, as a very short time sufficed to throw upwards of 700 men into the hospitals, and return 200 in a sort of convalescent state. I was among the latter number, that is to say, neither absolutely sick nor in health, and subject at times to fits of ague: sometimes a dozen men were to be seen shivering with this complaint at the same time in the barrack-room. As a preventive to the increase of the disease, we were often drawn up, and jugs of bark served out from rear to front. Three hundred of the guards,[16] who were sent over from South Beveland to our hospital, in a sickly state, died off nearly to a man; this constrained us to be continually engaged in the disgusting employment of burying them, as well as the dead of our own corps. A whole field had been completely filled with bodies when the

---

[14] The 84th (York and Lancaster) Foot.

[15] Often referred to as Walcheren Fever. Around 4,000 British troops died from a mixture of malaria, typhus and other waterborne and swamp-related diseases. A further 11,000 were stricken. Few made a full recovery. Just over 100 British soldiers were killed in battle. The 71st lost ninety men in the campaign, but only twenty-one of them were killed in action.

[16] All three Guards regiments in existence at the time were represented at Walcheren.

excessive fatigue of this occupation, united to our weakened constitutions, made it necessary afterwards for us to employ the inhabitants in the doleful service.

Little else but a succession of the same horrors occurred during our stay of three months in this den of pestilence.[17] We remarked that the town's people had carefully picked up the shells and rockets, which we had formerly thrown into the place while in possession of the French, and built them into the very apertures they had made in the walls of the houses. I presume the citizens intended that the warlike missives should thus stand conspicuously, as so many mementos to future generations, to show their forefathers' sufferings. I remember a story of some of our sailors, who belonged to one of the numerous guard boats which patrolled the coast, landing on the island of Beveland, and surprising a French picket, consisting of three men and a corporal. The sailors, not content with making them prisoners, burnt their guard house; and saying that it was a damned pity to take away the fellows without their house, the big children actually heaved a heavy sentry-box upon their shoulders, and brought it in along with the prisoners, groaning and sweating under the preposterous load.

Only a few days before our final evacuation of the island, I was attacked in a serious manner with the Walcheren sickness. To describe the torments of the ague cannot be interesting; however, I may state some of the sensations I felt: first, a sort of listlessness pervades the mind, accompanied with frequent yawning, the feet get cold, the cold then gradually ascends to the back, and in fact through the whole body; a universal icy shivering, and a chattering of the teeth, next ensue, followed by an ardent thirst; during the whole progress of the disorder the nails of the fingers are perfectly white. Two days before the regiment took its

---

[17] In November the regiment shipped 112 sick men back to England.

departure I was sent off to Flushing; embarking from thence in a small boat, to go out to the transport, I was attacked by severe fits of the ague, in consequence of the waves dashing over the vessel and wetting me to the skin. I was obliged to be hauled up the side of the transport nearly at the last gasp. After riding at anchor till the rest of the fleet was ready, we set sail for England, seeing first the docks and store-houses of Flushing set on flames, to prevent the enemy from reaping any advantage from them. While we were upwards of three miles from the Flanders shore, a 24 lb. ball came from a fort there, shattered our windlass, and, continuing its course, struck off a sergeant's legs in the head-quarter-ship![18]

On our arrival off Deal, I was placed, along with a number of other invalids, in a boat, to be towed ashore by another boat manned with sailors: before we had gone far, it was discovered that the plug was out, and that the water was rushing in upon us. It had risen already to our knees, when the sailor who steered jumped suddenly into the other boat among his comrades, under the pretext of getting us better towed. We soon perceived, however, that the heartless wretches were making preparations to cast off the towing line, and abandon us to our fate. The water was by this time up to the gunwale – the deep was yawning for its prey, and we felt by anticipation our dying struggles – when we were suddenly relieved from our despondency by one of our men starting up, loading his piece, and pointing it into the other boat: this kind of argument was irresistible to the '*gallant British tars*'; they instantly laid aside their villainous intentions, and the steersman came back with a very downcast look. A foraging cap was now stuffed into the leak, the plug was shortly after found, the towing was resumed, hope began to 'tell a flattering tale', till the beach was reached.

---

[18] This was probably actually Corporal James Steel. Despite the efforts of two surgeons, he died the following day.

When it was found that no small dexterity was required to land us, on account of a heavy surf beating on the shore. A party of soldiers belonging to a Welsh regiment was employed here to carry us ashore; this was performed by wading up to their middles, and lifting us on their backs. In this manner the whole party was landed safely, except four men, to wit, myself, two German soldiers, and another man – the boat having been unexpectedly driven on its side by a chance wave. It soon righted, however, but not without putting us in imminent jeopardy of our lives by drowning. We were at length dragged ashore like drowned rats, and placed in a waggon, to be carried to Deal. Just at that very moment, the inspiring notes of some well-known bugles burst on my ear; I could not be mistaken, the 71st had landed about the same time as myself, how much did I regret that there was no opportunity of joining them! But my debilitated state effectually prevented that.

I was now in the Deal hospital, where the greatest attention was paid me, particularly by an orderly man of the hospital, whom I discovered to be a native of Glasgow. He took me to his own ward, and administered to my wants with the utmost kindness and solicitude, during the whole time that I was in the place, which was three weeks. Such is the strange nature of mankind, that, merely because I drew my breath first among a certain heap of stones, another man, coming from the same heap, should do every thing in his power to serve me; whereas, had I unfortunately belonged to any other place, perhaps it would have stood hard with me, if I ever recovered.

It would, perhaps, be considered improper in me to dwell long in making remarks upon the hackneyed subjects of the folly of ministers in ordering such an invasion as that of Walcheren; the imbecility of the commander of the land forces; and the inexpediency of bombarding Flushing. That the expedition was miserably disastrous, both in the loss of lives among the soldiers, and in the waste of money to the nation, no one can deny. But it is doing no more than justice to the planners of it to say that they had not the remotest idea of the banefulness of the climate, although so near it – a fact unexampled in history; and this, as it is well known, was the primary cause of our ill success. As to the general, I believe he did every thing in his power to fulfil his orders; with the exception, perhaps, of being rather dilatory. The bombardment of Flushing was, in my humble opinion, preferable to the dreadful effects of storming the place.

It is also superfluous to descant upon the manners and customs of the Dutch; the contiguousness of their country to England would form of itself a palpable reason for this. For instance, their universal habit of cleanliness, and their practice of smoking tobacco, are well known even to the most illiterate people.

I now joined the regiment at Braeburnlees; but finding myself still unwell, I obtained leave of absence for three months, and went home to Glasgow. The ague continued to stick close by me nearly the whole time I was there. An old sailor advised me to take some brandy mixed with gunpowder; it might be imagination, but after swallowing this rough medicine, I found myself gradually getting better.

Leaving old Glasgow once more, I returned to the south. Coming up in the London smack, two hours after leaving Leith, one of the passengers entered into a conversation with me, inquiring if I had been at Walcheren, the number of my regiment, whether I would like best to be a sailor or a soldier, and such like chit-chat. The steward at this time calling the cabin passengers to tea, the stranger went down along with them, but soon came up again, carrying a porringer of tea and a roll – these he politely forced me to accept. Next day, another passenger, who had the appearance of an English traveller, tired, seemingly, with the monotony of a sea life, challenged, for a pastime, any of the company to ascend to the mast-head with him; none but the stranger took him up. They both accordingly climbed to the very top; but, in conformity to the usual custom, two sailors mounted after them, and tied the traveller to the mast, where he hung, the laughing-stock of every passenger, until he promised to pay a bottle of rum to the crew.[19] The traveller now came down, I dare say rather nettled at the issue of his exploit, and at the stranger for not being tied up also. I was not near enough to distinguish every word, but I could plainly discover that high words were likely to ensue between the climbers; this, however, was suddenly put a stop to, by the steward whispering into the traveller's ear, that he was speaking to Lord Cochrane.[20] The Englishman was dumb instantly: – such is the effect of a title, a great name, or the possession of money, that even the most independent-spirited man is involuntarily awed for a time by such advantages, although he may be in the right. It was through these means that I found out that my generous and truly noble entertainer, and Lord Cochrane, were one and the same person.

Having again joined the regiment at Braeburnlees, we marched off to Deal, where we lay till the month of September; 600 of the most effective men in the regiment

---

[19] Passengers on sailing ships carrying emigrants to Australia and New Zealand right up until at the least the 1840s reported they faced a similar rum forfeit if they were caught in the rigging by a crew member.

[20] Scots-born Thomas Cochrane was regarded as one of the leading British sailors of his time. He was known as the 'Sea Wolf'. He was also a prolific inventor and filed fourteen patent applications, including ones for the manufacture of coal gas, a rotary steam engine and a screw propulsion system for ships. He also investigated the possibilities of the military use of poison gas. But he was a controversial figure and was jailed for his alleged part in a stock-market fraud which involved giving a false report of Napoleon's death to boost share prices. Cochrane would command the Chilean navy between 1818 and 1822, the Brazilian navy from 1823 to 1825 and the Greek navy between 1827 and 1828.

were then picked out to serve in the Peninsula:[21] the rest of the corps had not yet recovered from the effects of their Walcheren trip. I was thought efficient enough to be enrolled among the former number. Our commander was by this time changed, Colonel Pack having gone into the Portugueze service: the command was now jointly swayed by the Colonels Peacock and Reynolds.[22]

---

[21] The men were mustered into six companies. A battalion at this time was made up of ten companies. A survey of the entire strength of the 71st while it was still stationed in England revealed it was composed of 701 Scots, 287 Irishmen and 69 Englishmen. The regimental rolls in those days did not always distinguish between Englishmen and Welshmen.

[22] The latter officer referred to was the American-born Major Thomas Reynell. He was to command the 71st at the Battle of Waterloo. In later life, he would marry the widow of the 71st's former commanding officer Sir Denis Pack. Lieutenant Colonel Nathan Peacock reportedly did not take well to the rigors of life on campaign and was happy to relinquish command of the 71st's 1st Battalion to Lieutenant Colonel Henry Cadogan. Peacock is sometimes spelled Peacocke.

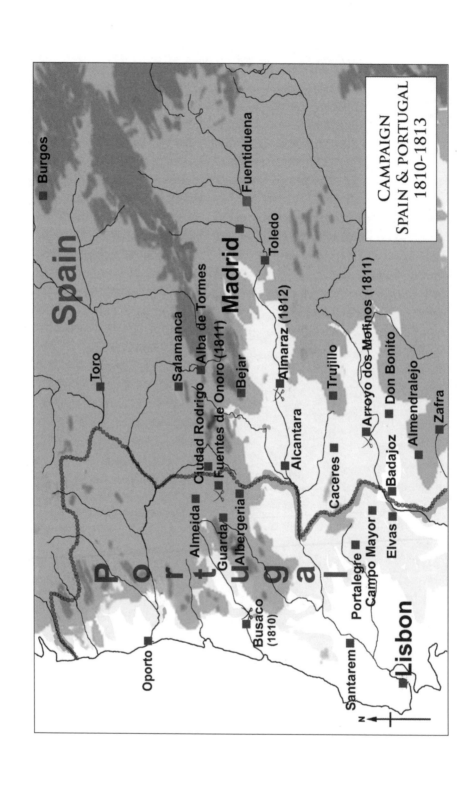

CAMPAIGN
SPAIN & PORTUGAL
1810-1813

Spain

Portugal

Burgos

Toro

Salamanca

Alba de Tormes

Ciudad Rodrigo

Fuentes de Onoro (1811)

Bejar

Madrid

Fuentiduena

Toledo

Almaraz (1812)

Trujillo

Arroyo dos Molinos (1811)

Don Bonito

Almendralejo

Zafra

Alcantara

Caceres

Badajoz

Elvas

Campo Mayor

Portalegre

Almeida

Guarda

Albergeria

Busaco (1810)

Oporto

Santarem

Lisbon

N

Chapter Four

Two frigates having been appointed to take us out, we embarked at Deal, and sailed next morning. This voyage was as prosperous as could be expected – fourteen days' sailing enabling us to land at Black-horse Square, Lisbon, on the 28th of September, 1810. We lay some days in the city; camp equipage was then served out, the soldiers' wives who had children were all obliged to remain, express orders being given to that effect. Having been thus freed from all unnecessary impediments, we marched up the country to join that army which had been reaping its laurels at Talavera, about the very time we were sailing to fill the fenny graves of Walcheren.

Arriving at Mafra, a palace belonging to the king of Portugal, we were quartered in it for a few days. The sergeants, who were sent before us to allot the different lodgings to the men, found the upper apartments swarming with such hosts of fleas, that when we entered the place, we beheld the sergeants stripped naked, banging their clothes against the walls, in order to shake out these petty but troublesome enemies. It was then found absolutely necessary for us to evacuate the best places in the house, and retire to the ground flat, where there was a stone floor, – resigning thus, for comfort's sake, every idea of contending longer with the fleas; no doubt a wonderful triumph to the insect world over armed men.

About this time Colonel Cadogan[1] joined us, having been appointed to the command of the regiment. He made an animating speech to us on this occasion, the substance of which was his satisfaction at obtaining the command of our 'heroic corps', a command which he had long ardently panted for, his hopes of having the honour to lead us on to higher achievements than we had ever yet performed, and so on.

Continuing our march, we fell in with immense numbers of the unfortunate Portugueze people, who had been literally turned out of house and hall; they were travelling towards Lisbon, as the only place of refuge from the baleful influence of the contending armies. A large tract of country had been laid waste, and their houses desolated, to prevent the French from receiving supplies in the pursuit of our army, which it seems was retreating with rapid strides towards the coast. The wretched and emaciated looks of the Portugueze travellers were truly piteous to a feeling heart; some of them were mounted on cars, such as the sick and children; but by far the greater number were crawling painfully along on their feet. I particularly remarked many frail old women endeavouring to support their tottering steps with staffs. The sufferings of many a British inhabitant have been, and are at times, great; but the above-mentioned sight convinced me that we have endured but little in comparison to the Portugueze. Unless

---

[1] The 30-year-old son of an Irish nobleman, Henry Cadogan was born in London and joined the 18th Foot, the Royal Irish, when he was 17 years old. He went on to serve in the Coldstream Guards and as an aide-de-camp to the Duke of Wellington before assuming command of the 1/71st. His sister Charlotte married Wellington's brother Henry, while another sister, Emily, married another of Wellington's brothers, Gerald. Although Cadogan never married, his son, also Henry, served with the 71st in the 1820s.

we go back as far as the times of Cromwell, the Pretender,[2] or prior to those unhappy periods, – our country has remained for a long time in happy ignorance of the real horrors of war.

We now saw Lord Wellington for the first time since the battle of Vimiera; and soon after we arrived at the town of Sobral. Here we met our army in full retreat from the field of Busaco; this battle had been fought only two days before we landed in Portugal. A woful change had taken place in the appearance of Sobral since I saw it last; then a more beautiful or lively place never existed; but now the houses were gutted, the gardens destroyed, and the busy hum of its former inhabitants hushed: a half-starved hog or two might occasionally be seen stealing along the deserted streets; but these, with an old crippled woman, who could not make her escape, and a cat, were the only natives of the place to be found. However, as part of the army (our own regiment was in the number) took up quarters for the night in the town, the solemn stillness was soon dissolved; military bustle is well calculated to banish all romantic reflections.

Towards the close of next day, the enemy made their appearance: we were purposely left alone to engage them, being supposed to be fresher than the rest of the army, who were much knocked up by their laborious retreat. Perhaps it might also have been intended that we should come in for a share of the fighting, and make up our lee-way in that respect. Notwithstanding our best efforts to the contrary, the Frenchmen drove us out of the town, though not without a good deal of difficulty; they at length retreated in their turn. We bivouacked that night mid-way between the French and British armies, but marched back in the

---

[2] Oliver Cromwell and either of the Stuart pretenders to the British throne in the 1700s – James or his son Charles Edward, better known as Bonnie Prince Charlie.

morning, and occupied Sobral again. Half of our company was now sent out on picket; I remained along with the other half, in a house where a quantity of dried fish was found; this, in addition to plenty of rice and Indian corn, contributed materially to making us all very merry: for the immediate prospect of meat draws forth cheerfulness at once from hungry men. An oven being in the place, many set to and baked abundance of bread, not only with the intention of filling their bellies but their haversacks besides; our 'here to-day and gone to-morrow', sort of life, putting us under the necessity of breaking the Christian mandate of 'take no heed for to-morrow'. But, alas! we were unexpectedly roused from these intellectual enjoyments by orders to turn out and join the picket on the outside of the town. Catching up our firelocks with some reluctance, we issued forth, and effected the junction. Scarcely had we done so, when General Erskine[3] rode up, and ordered us to retreat, as the enemy were advancing. By the time we had retraced our steps back to the town, we found the rest of the regiment drawn up under arms: the general then ordered two companies to post themselves on a neighbouring hill, which was thickly covered with vines. The intention of this was to amuse the enemy, as it were, while we were effecting our escape. The French, both infantry and cavalry, were by this time nearly close to us. They presented a numerous and imposing front; – we were, therefore, again obliged to suffer ourselves to be driven

---

[3] Sir William Erskine was insane. When the Duke of Wellington protested against the Scot's appointment he was told in a communication from Whitehall: 'No doubt he is a little mad at times, but in his lucid moments he is an uncommonly clever fellow and I trust he will have no fit during the campaign, though I must say he looked a little mad as he embarked.' He was also almost blind. After a series of battlefield blunders he was on the verge of being sent home when he threw himself out of a window in Lisbon. As he lay dying he asked, 'Why on earth did I do that?'

through the town at double quick time. Hurrying past the house we had left with so much regret, one of us ran in at a venture, and brought out a loaf from the oven, at the expense of a burnt hand.

At length we halted from our race at the outside of the town; the two companies soon after made their appearance, closely pursued by the French. The vine trees which they had to force through in their flight had the usual peculiarity of catching a tenacious hold of any person who presumes to invade their territories, especially if he is in haste. This being the case with our comrades, it was with some difficulty that they surmounted the obstacles which both the French and the vines threw in their way. They now joined us, having, upon the whole, covered our retreat with great skill and succeeded in attracting much of the enemy's attention. Just as they came up to us, one of them received a ball from the French, in some part or other of his body, the sudden smart of which made him spring up several feet in the air, in the same manner that a cock does. We were inconsiderate enough to raise a horse laugh at the man's misfortune, but this was rather at the oddity of his behaviour in receiving it.

The enemy having for the present ceased hostilities, we bivouacked for the night in a ploughed field; no comfortable bed, indeed, considering that we had, in addition, a high wind and frequent showers of rain. Next day, having got on our greatcoats and bonnet covers, the enemy attacked us with greater vigour and resolution than ever. We heard afterwards that this extraordinary fierceness was occasioned by their taking us for Portugueze, on account of our change of dress: it is necessary to say here, that the French had hitherto been accustomed to drive the Portugueze like sheep before them. A continual skirmishing was kept up the whole day, from behind walls and other places of ambush. At one time, the enemy came on in such overwhelming numbers, that we were obliged to retreat rather precipitately over a wall. One of our men, named Rae,[4] a native of Paisley, and the oldest man in the regiment, not being so active in ascending the wall as the rest of us, and perhaps being apprehensive of receiving a bayonet thrust *par derriere* while doing so, he chose courageously to stand his ground alone: the first enemy that approached he shot dead, the next he bayoneted, a third shared the same fate – and the ancient hero then coolly effected his retreat. Another man, while coming over the wall, received no less than a dozen of bullets through his greatcoat and canteen, without suffering a single wound in any part of his body. But another poor fellow did not escape so well; he had, for security's sake, cunningly pulled as many stones out of the wall as would admit the barrel of his musket. While he was in a crouching attitude, preparing to keep up an incessant fire on the enemy from his loop-hole, a ball came from them, and, by a remarkable accident, entered the very aperture and his eye at the same instant, leaving him dead on the spot. Before the heat of the engagement came on, we were honoured with a visit from an officer who had held, not long before, a high rank in the regiment. We were rather surprised at his unusual boldness in coming without compulsion to a place where there was danger, as it had hitherto been notorious to us all, that when there was any thing like fighting in the case, the gentleman in question would rather have been in Lapland. But our wavering doubts of his returning courage were soon dissipated, in consequence of two or three balls from the French whistling through the air. This unexpected salute so petrified the unhappy hero, that he cried to us in a palpitating voice, 'He was afraid his *horse* would be shot.' Looking round then, and dreading the approach of more leaden-almonds, he told us to tell Colonel Cadogan that 'he had called upon him'; so saying, he

---

[4] Rae does not appear to have been much liked. Gavin in his diary described him as a useless burden on the regiment.

galloped off like lightning amidst the sneers of the soldiery. Perhaps, after all, such a man as this deserves pity rather than contempt.

General Erskine and Colonel Cadogan, having been eye-witnesses of Rae's bravery, afterwards ordered him to be presented with a medal, bearing the following inscription:

To JOHN RAE,
for his exemplary courage and good
conduct as a Soldier, at Sobral,
14th October, 1810.

He also had the offer of being appointed to the rank of a sergeant, but this he refused: he was a man of a gloomy disposition; in short, a Methodist.[5] It is remarkable enough, that the medal was made out of a common dollar, by one of the men, in a manner which would have done no discredit to the best silversmith: this man had never been bred to such a profession, but was of an ingenious turn in all respects. The din of war having ended, we now got time to look around us. It was found, in the first place, that the ploughed field we stood upon had got so wet with the heavy rain, that it was with difficulty any one could walk over it. No sooner was one foot dragged forward, than the other sunk deep, and stuck fast in the soil: in fact, our appearance could, without exaggeration, have been compared to that of bees among tar. One man, who, I presume, had been a weaver, tormented by the pains of his former fatigue, and the annoyance of his present state, was heard to exclaim, that he would rather be working an '*eight and twa*' at home than be at this work.

---

[5] Many soldiers who were labelled 'Methodists' earned the soubriquet for their strict moral standards and were not necessarily members of the Methodist Church.

When the sun had sunk beneath the horizon, or, in other words, when it was dark, we retreated over a hill where a fort was situated. The fort's proper name I know not, but among us it went by the name of the Black Battery: this was the utmost point which the enemy advanced to, in the direction of Lisbon, at this time. We now arrived at a village, where we took up our quarters. We were joined at this place by the 50th and 92nd regiments, which had just landed in Portugal. Continuing our progress, we arrived and halted at Sobreira; the enemy had by this time occupied Sobral, which being only a mile distant from us, consequently the enemy's sentinels and our own were quite close to each other. Constant employment was now given us as labourers. We were engaged in cutting down, for instance, many orange groves to build breast-works, or, properly speaking, assisting in the formation of those famous lines[6] which baffled the skill and utmost efforts of Massena[7] to penetrate.

The lines being completely finished, we lay in sight of the enemy for six weeks. Few important events took place all that while. Having little to do, we sometimes employed ourselves in searching for corn which the Portugueze had hid under ground: our system of doing this was to find out a particular place where the ground sounded hollow at the stamp of a foot. When such a discovery was made, a ramrod was driven down to prove the presence of the grain: by these means great quantities were often found. A house which lay between the enemy's picket and our own was greatly famed for containing a good store of wine, which of course had no owner, or at least nobody knew or cared where he was: the news of this drew bibbers of both armies in flocks to the

---

[6] The Lines of Torres Vedras.

[7] Andrea Massena was another former army private promoted to marshal by Napoleon. Wellington described him as the 'most dangerous and difficult' of Napoleon's generals he faced. He was commander of the Army of Portugal 1810–11. His mistress reputedly accompanied him on campaign disguised in a dragoon's uniform.

place. Many were to be seen slipping cautiously out to evade the observation of the sentinels, and repairing to the general rendezvous: a form of politeness was kept up even there – the British waiting on the outside of the house till the French soldiers had satisfied themselves with the 'rosy wine'; they then went in to the same work, while the French waited in their turn to renew the attack. Before the road to this house had been universally known, some of our men met a Highlander returning from it, half-seas-over: they asked him several questions, such as, if the liquor was good; but the only reply that could be drawn from Donald was, 'that it is *sin but thousands o't'*, meaning thereby, that the wine was thin, but there was plenty of it.

One day, some of the men being put in search of oranges, a young Irish lad, one of the party, fell by some means or other into the hands of the French. Some time after this, in the course of the enemy's retreat, we found him extended on the road, so reduced by hunger, sickness, and fatigue, that nobody knew him, not even his own brother who was also in the regiment. The poor wretch was at last only recognised by some marks on his clothes: he died, however, soon afterwards.

Another day I saw Marshal Massena come down pretty near us, accompanied only by two or three of his staff: he was apparently reconnoitering our position, taking several peeps through a telescope in our direction. Although the Marshal was completely within our reach, no one thought of firing at him, as we knew that the French would be as honourable as ourselves in this respect, if they had the same opportunity. At the end of six weeks, as I said before, the enemy relinquished their blockade, and decamped in the night-time, without beat of drum in consequence of their provisions being entirely exhausted. It was the middle of the following day before we discovered their retreat; the lines were in consequence evacuated with great speed, and an immediate pursuit commenced.

While we were passing hurriedly through the town of Sobral once more, some legible chalked letters on the door met our eyes – they were to this effect – 'two of the 71st here': some of us went accordingly into the house, and found two of our men who had been taken prisoners by the French; both of the unfortunate fellows were disabled by the loss of a leg each. The humane attention of the enemy in guiding us to their assistance deserves some applause: I question if the warriors of any nation but the French and British would have had the generosity to perform such an action.

In the course of the pursuit, a party of our cavalry captured some French prisoners and brought them in to deliver them to the charge of Colonel Cadogan. A sergeant was sent along with them, to point out the way to the colonel's quarters. While the sergeant was doing this, walking at the head of the cavalcade, he fell accidentally into a draw-well. This occurrence alarmed the prisoners, who supposed that the sudden vanishing of the unfortunate guide was a trick to decoy them to an untimely end: however, he was hauled out, after having stood for some time up to the chin in water.

After continuing the pursuit for some days, our headquarters were established at Cartaxo, the enemy having halted at Santarem with the resolution of standing their ground. We then marched to the vicinity of the latter place in expectation of giving battle; but it was soon discovered that the French had posted themselves in such an advantageous position, that any effort of ours to dislodge them would be ineffectual. We lay before the town a whole day, during which time Colonel Cadogan, with the intention of creating amusement, set every trade in the regiment to run races with each other; the victors were rewarded with rum: the tailors and shoemakers,[8] I recollect, had a keen contest.

---

[8] Although the bulk of the regiment were either ex-weavers or ex-labourers, there were usually four to six tailors or shoemakers in each company.

In the evening we marched to a village, to take up quarters: through some mistake, a party of us and a party of the 92nd were told off, or billeted, on the same house. Fortunately for us, we had taken possession of it first, as it was not long till the 92nd party appeared, demanding admittance, and, commanding us in an imperious tone, to turn out. This hard condition was absolutely refused, it being a very wet rough night; upon which they sent for their Colonel, thinking, no doubt, to terrify us into submission by this means. But on his arrival, our officer answered his blustering threats by sternly repeating our fixed deter- mination to remain where we were. Finding that it was impossible to effect an entrance, they quietly retreated, to roost in some other place; where, I know not. Our excitation had been so great, that I verily believe blood would have been shed ere our expulsion could have been effected.[9] Next day we marched to Almastairs and were quartered there in a nunnery and a convent contiguous to one another.

Truly, little respect was paid here to the sanctity of the Catholic religion by the men; many of them were to be seen washing their shirts in the holy water fonts; one fellow also took the wooden image of a saint, and threw it into a fire which was kindled at the chapel door, crying at the same time, 'Down with popery!' A Highland officer belonging to the 92nd happened unluckily to enter at the time, and seeing this, was so shocked and scandalised at the supposed sacrilege of the action (being a Catholic himself) that he

---

[9] The Highland Light Infantry and their fellow Scots in the 92nd Gordon Highlanders had a sometimes uneasy relationship. During the 1808 campaign, the Gordons noticed that the local Spanish population was inclined to give them the cold shoulder. It emerged that the Spanish speakers in the HLI, who picked the language up during their imprisonment in Argentina, had been telling the local population that the Gordons were forced to wear skirts as a punishment for their misdeeds. The Gordons complained and several of the HLI men were punished for slandering their kilted colleagues.

expressed himself to this effect: '*You seventy-furst will cum to a pad end one tay.*'[10] The French had only evacuated the nunnery the night before our arrival; they had, with the mischievous taste of monkeys, torn and destroyed a number of books and papers belonging to the nuns, and, in short, turned every thing topsy-turvy. It must be owned, however, that we were not backward in completing the work of destruction, as all the movable furniture was broken down and used up for our fire-wood.

All thoughts of disturbing the enemy at Santarem being given up for the present, we moved on to the deserted village of Alcintrina, and there took up our winter quarters. The weather being cold, and having nothing to shelter ourselves but the naked walls of the houses, we were put to great shifts for the sake of snugness at night; we had then to take off part of our clothes, to serve as a kind of couches, counterpanes were formed by greatcoats, and our legs being thrust through the sleeves gave additional warmth. Our time in this place was passed rather monotonously; however, every kind of amusement that we could invent was put in practice. The officers often exercised themselves by riding horse and ass races; games of football and cricket[11] were also instituted; besides occasional dances, to the sound of the bagpipe. At other times, we had recourse to our old plan of proving the ground with ramrods: corn and clothes were generally the fruits of our labour; but at one time something like a box was felt. Fired with the hope of gold, or some other rich prize, all around fell to digging up the earth; but, alas! when the object of our search was exposed to view, it proved to be a coffin, containing the body of a Portugueze. The place being at some distance from any burying-ground, we were the more surprised at

[10] The 92nd Highlanders contained a fair proportion of Catholics, recruited from western Inverness-shire.

[11] The regiment had formed a cricket club during their 1806–1807 sojourn in South America as prisoners of war.

the discovery; in fact, it is the universal custom of that country to bury the dead under churches. However, without questioning whether the knife of the assassin, or the excommunication of the priest, had caused the corpse to be placed here, we closed the coffin, and put it into its former situation, leaving the ashes to moulder, unseen more by mortal eye.

At length, about the beginning of March 1811, the enemy retreated from their strong position at Santarem. In consequence of this, we broke up our quarters, and joined in the pursuit, passing by the way through the village of Torres Novas. Every day the advanced guard of our army and the enemy's rear-guard were engaged. The miserable effects of a rapid retreat began already to be visible. We were continually passing over the bodies of men and horses who had been slain, wounded, or knocked up by fatigue; but not one of the human beings was alive in consequence of the crowds of cowardly Portugueze ruffians who were hanging constantly on the way, killing and stripping every man that lay helpless on the ground. This was all done under the specious pretence of patriotism, and the desire of avenging the injuries they had received from the French. But the true nature of these jackals was soon discovered, and the direct lie given to their patriotic professions, by their murdering indiscriminately every Briton, as well as Frenchman, who was so unfortunate as to be unable to offer resistance; besides, all of them carried large sacks to contain the spoils of the victims. We got so exasperated at the conduct of these fellows, that they, for security's sake, always carried on their unhallowed work at a respectful distance from us.

However, it must be owed, that the French retaliated in the most cruel manner; and, it is more than probable, the innocent, not the guilty, were the chief sufferers. Every house and village we came to was found in flames, and the

91

fate of their inhabitants was horrible to the last degree. Scott,[12] in his *Vision of Don Roderick*, describes their miseries thus:–

> O, triumph for the fiends of lust and wrath!
> Ne'er to be told, yet ne'er to be forgot,
> What wanton horrors mark'd their wrackful path!
> The peasant butchered in his ruined cot,
> The hoary priest even at the altar shot,
> Childhood and age given o'er to sword and flame,
> Woman to infamy; – no crime forgot.
> By which inventive demons might proclaim
> Immortal hate to man, and scorn of God's great name!
> The rudest sentinel, in Britain born,
> With horror paused to view the havoc done,
> Gave his poor crust to feed some wretch forlorn,
> Wiped his stern eye, then fiercer grasped his gun.

Such was the extremity of hunger among the Portugueze, that it was common to see them eagerly picking up and eating the grains of corn at the places where cavalry horses were fed. Having arrived at the town of Pombal, where a part of the army was engaged, we continued advancing. The awful spectacle of the whole town of Condacia in flames next engaged our attention: this place appears to have been a fashionable resort of the Portugueze nobility and gentry, the houses being all stately and magnificent; but a sad change was rapidly taking place – a devouring fire raging unchecked on both sides of the streets as we marched through.

I have no wish to extenuate the excesses of the French army in this retreat; – on the contrary, I think I felt just as much for the Portugueze as the common run of people did: yet there are some circumstances which ought to be

---

[12] Scottish writer Sir Walter Scott.

recollected. Had the British been placed in the same, predicament as the French were, – that is to say, had they been the enemies and invaders of Portugal, they would have found it to be a very different thing from being friendly allies; they would have found that they had to contend with a treacherous and ferocious set of people; who neglected no means, however base or unworthy, to cut off an inoffensive straggling soldier; besides having, in addition, to cope with an army of foreigners as valiant as themselves. These grievances would have, in consequence, roused and goaded them on to revenge. The nature of war also having a tendency to render the heart callous and to brutify the mind, they would, excited by blind fury, have been induced to go farther in their retaliation than the rules of justice prescribed. In short, I have little hesitation in saying, that the British would have committed the same enormities as the French did, had they been in the same situation. Another thing is, the French army was far from being composed wholly of Frenchmen; – the unceasing wars of Buonaparte had drained France of men, the deficiencies were therefore made up out of conquered countries, such as Germany and Italy – consequently the natives of these countries were mercenaries, having no cause to fight for: as whatever victory they might contribute to gain, they knew that the French alone would have all the credit. They therefore determined that their masters should have all the odium too, so that there is little doubt but that the mercenaries were thus the principal perpetrators of the before-mentioned cruelties. Away then with our vulgar prejudices against the French: let us look at our proceedings in India, or in the American war, where Germans were also employed;[13]

---

[13] German mercenaries, many from Hesse-Kassel, were employed by the British during the American Revolution of 1775–83. The first contingents arrived in 1776. The use of foreign troops against English-speaking colonists proved controversial on both sides of the Atlantic.

having done so, it is highly hypocritical to exclaim against the French in the present case, or to say more than deplore in general the deteriorating effects of war.

After leaving Condacia, we were destitute of provisions for three days, the country being in manner eaten up: the usual allowance of rum was still being served out, however, – but empty stomachs and ardent spirits do not agree well together. In short, a moderate quantity was sufficient to render a person intoxicated, and this was the case with the most of us. The enemy were also reduced to such straits for meat, that they were obliged to feed on ass and horse flesh; the skins of the asses were often to be seen lying on the road, and the carcass of almost every dead horse we passed by had either one or both hips cut off: to judge by appearance, that part of the horse must be the most savoury – none of us, however, knew by experience.

Coming up one night with the enemy's rear, the light division of our army engaged them, but they retired precipitately over the river Ceira, blowing up the bridge, to stop the pursuit; a number of the enemy, who were still on it, lost their lives in consequence of the explosion being performed too hastily. That night we saw a number of asses which had been hamstrung: if they had not been suffering excruciating agony, we should have been tempted to laugh at the droll contortions of the poor creatures, – they lay huddled together among some mud, and whenever any person approached, a general kicking and sprawling took place.

In bivouacking at this place, we had to endure the combined miseries of a wet night and hunger. Next morning, one of the men who had been foraging brought in a bag of Indian corn: with this inestimable treasure he generously went round the whole company, giving each of us a handful. Soon after this, three days' allowance of beef were served out, which quickly restored hilarity, and kept the cooks and jaws hard at work for the remainder of the day. The blowing up of the bridge had retarded our advance for two days; but on a ford being discovered, we crossed the river on the 17th of March, and continued our march for two successive days. We then halted again, for the estimable purpose of refreshing ourselves: the word was rather misplaced, considering that we had nothing to eat – it being generally allowed that meat constitutes no inconsiderable part of refreshment to hungry men. About this time we were regaled by Lord Wellington reviewing us.

Any little savings the men had made were now obliged to be thrown away in purchasing something to stay the gnawing of their stomachs, – often I have seen a private pay a dollar for a small biscuit, thinking himself happy to get it at any price. This time enabled the butchers of the army to reap a golden harvest, they having the offals of all the bullocks they slew as perquisites: the most nauseating garbage was sold at enormous prices. The greasy rogues, knowing their power, held tenaciously at the prices they had laid down; and rather than do otherwise, they would some-times actually go and bury the carrion under ground. Many of the men were detected herein stealing honey from some hives in the neighbourhood; the colonel discovered the thieves by looking for all those who had their faces stung by the bees: the culprits were punished by extra pickets, or a temporary stoppage of their rum: – but surely it should have been recollected that necessity is all-powerful.

Continuing our march through the north of Portugal, we began to observe that the country was getting more and more barren, and that every house was in a state of beastly filth. Happening to be billeted on a house along with some others, its loathsome Augean-stable-like appearance had nearly saved the inmates the trouble of entertaining us: however, concealing our disgust as much as possible, in the same manner as the wolf did in the ape's den, we entered. Stepping towards the fire-place to dress our victuals, the black ferocious-looking landlord called to us not to set our

95

feet upon his mother: astonished at this warning, no person being apparently in sight of that description, we looked round more particularly, and discovered something in the form of a human being lying crumpled up in the corner of the ash-pit, which was a step lower than the floor: it was with great difficulty we could believe that it was one of our own species before our eyes, she actually being little larger than a full-grown hen! The host told us that she had lain for upwards of thirty years in the ash-pit, nearly in the same position; age, therefore, not a dwarfish nature, had reduced the creature to a diminutive size, and the strange attitude undoubtedly had materially helped to effect the same. After this time, having no wish to intrude on the privacies of such people, we went out of doors and cooked.

Arriving at the village of Salorica,[14] some of the men went out secretly to 'search the ground', as it was called: – this practice had of late become very common, although dis-countenanced by strict commands to the contrary; but, with regard to this party, they had not searched long till they came upon a jar. Thinking, of course, that it would, without doubt, contain money, the sages unanimously agreed not to lift the treasure till the shades of night should allow them to do so with more security. Marking the place, therefore, they returned, planning likely as much future happiness as the barber's brother in the Arabian Nights. The discovery was too important, however, to allow them to be mute; through this means an additional partner to the enterprise was obtained. It seems that a sergeant, remarkable in the regiment only for his low cunning, had overheard their golden discourse; and no sooner had the treasure-seekers sallied forth, at the time agreed on, than he followed on tiptoe, taking the utmost care not to disturb them until the precious jar was disinterred, and fully exposed to the greedy gaze of their wondering eyes, – then indeed he stept

---

[14] Sometimes written as Celerico.

forward, with a benevolent smile on his countenance, and modestly claimed only two or three shares of what was found. The party were at first rather disconcerted at the unexpected honour of a visit from a non-commissioned officer on such an errand; but, considering that there still would be enough to make them all, they bore up under the misfortune with some equanimity. But who can describe their sensations when the jar was uncorked, to find that it only contained some fine olive oil: – perhaps the tearing of hair, the gnashing of teeth, and cursing the hour of their birth, did not ensue, – but the woe of the horror-struck crew was great. Envious fortune, however, had not yet expended their quiver of misfortunes, – as at the very time they thought their misery was wound up to the highest pitch, they were suddenly surprised and taken prisoners by a sergeant who had orders to look out for all 'proggers'. The cunning sergeant was disgraced for this offence, by being reduced to the ranks, notwithstanding his protestations of innocence. One of the excuses was he was not of the party; but this defence did not pass, so he found he had over-reached himself for once.

In the course of this march we had another example of villainous hypocrisy, – a sergeant having officiously found fault with a man for pilfering a little flour from a Portugueze family: he lectured the culprit in the severest terms, upon the heinous sin of plundering the poor starving people: 'You should,' said he, 'rather have given them a portion of your own provisions, than have been so base-minded as to rob them of their last morsel.' This was all very well, every one concurring heartily in the honourable sentiments of the worthy sergeant; and already he was set down as a very saint among us: – but what was our surprise, on resuming our march, to see the canteen strap of the man of stripes break by accident, and discover to our astonished eyes the identical flour pouring out on the road. Not daring to charge him openly with the gross deceit, loud murmuring was heard on every side repeating his very words, such as 'you should have given and not robbed,' &c. The hypocrite, on hearing the just reproof, slunk aside, without saying a single syllable, knowing well what was meant. Thus it appeared, that the moment the original thief had put back the flour to the place from whence it was taken; our worthy had gone and stolen it himself: I should have said before, that he had ordered the man to return the flour to the injured people.

Leaving Portugal we entered Spain and soon after arrived at the town of Albergeria; a visible change for the better took place in the appearance of the country, the houses and the people, immediately after crossing the frontier. The war had raised the price of some articles to an enormous pitch at this place; common salt, for instance, sold at 3s a pound, and tobacco at 7s; other things in proportion. The arrival of the commissary with provisions was at all times looked on as an event of the last importance: he having to go as far as Lisbon for these necessaries, of course the farther we receded from the coast, the farther were his journeys, and the longer the time occupied in performing them. A plain extended for some leagues round the town of Albergeria; and often did we catch the first glimpse of the provision mules. When they did arrive, the very brutes appeared of consequence in our eyes; but the commissary was considered almost as an angel of light. Such are the effects of spare diet upon the minds of hungry men!

Having frequent dealings in the market-place with Spanish hucksters, we often had our risibility excited by the rogueries of a long lean Irishman belonging to the regiment. This fellow, finding the Spaniards apt to be easily gulled, immediately made proposals to sell their articles for them to us, under the plausible pretext of seeing justice done to both sides. His services were accepted; by which means he contrived to cheat the unsuspecting people every day of a good round sum of money, besides receiving a handsome commission for his trouble. From the gay deceiver's appearance, the Spaniards nicknamed him *Pacalarga,* which, literally translated, means *long-straw.* The whole time we lay in place Pacalarga carried on his pranks with such secrecy and success, that scarcely a bargain could be concluded upon, without his advice being first taken by the honest Albergerians.

Chapter Five

The enemy having resumed the offensive, we quitted our cantonment, and arrived on the plains of Fuentes de Honoro[1] on the 3rd May: part of our army had already come in contact with the foe, but we were employed first only in manœuvering. This kind of labour was held in universal detestation by the men; principally on account of never seeing any advantage arise from it.

Passing over a field of garlic in one of our many tacks, some of the men thought it proper to regale themselves on this loathsome vegetable, and their comrades were in a short time almost suffocated with the smell of their breath. This caused the garlic-eaters to be assailed with many oaths and curses; but threatening sorts of words were so common-place among soldiers, that all their terrors are regarded as little as the 'playful zephyr'. Permission was at length given for us to stretch our wearied limbs upon the ground, the officers then went out a short distance to have a nearer view of the engagement going on.

---

[1] The placename is rendered as Fuentes D'Onor on the regimental colour. It is also sometimes spelled Fuentes d'Onoro , Fuentes de Onoro or Fuentes Onoro.

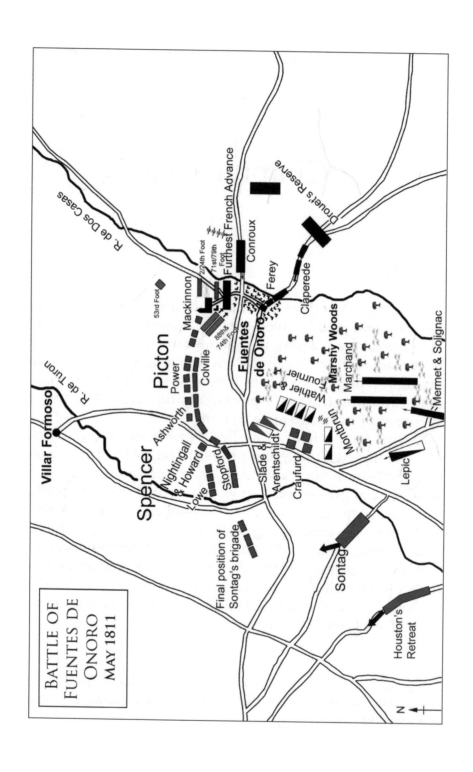

BATTLE OF
FUENTES DE
ONORO
MAY 1811

R. de Dos Casas

R. de Turon

Villar Formoso

Spencer

Picton

53rd Foot

Power

Mackinnon

Colville

88th & 74th Foot

2/24th Foot

71st/79th Foot

Furthest French Advance

Conroux

Ferey

Claperede

Fuentes de Onoro

Ashworth

Nightingall & Howard

Lowe

Stopford

Slade & Arentschildt

Craufurd

Final position of Sontag's brigade

Montbrun

Wathier & Fournier

Marshy Woods

Marchand

Mermet & Solignac

Lepic

Sontag

Houston's Retreat

Drouet's Reserve

N

We were soon roused, by the coming up of General Spenser[2] with orders for us to advance to the scene of the action. 'Come my lads,' said Colonel Cadogan, 'you are to get biscuit and rum served out in the village', concluding the speech thus in his own peculiar laconic manner. Three men out of each company in the regiment were at this time assisting the wounded of the engaged regiments; they had left their arms and accoutrements behind; we were therefore necessitated to divide, and carry them forward by turns. The old treasure-seeking incident sergeant and myself had for our share of luggage a heavy knapsack between us. As we were rapidly approaching the enemy, they opened fire upon us from some pieces of cannon; one of the balls struck the ground a yard or two to the right of our company, going in such a direction that it was very near sweeping the whole of us down. Arriving at the village of Fuentes, we saw twelve light companies which had been repeatedly driven out of it by the enemy, though they had displayed prodigious valour.[3] The musketry of the French began already to be felt among us, several of the men falling down wounded. At a time like this, the bearing of an extra knapsack being an insupportable annoyance to us two, we inquired of an officer what was to be done with it: 'Carry it still, to be sure,' was the reply.

---

[2] Lieutenant General Brent Spencer was Wellington's second-in-command in 1808 and 1810–11. Wellington regarded him as brave but 'exceedingly puzzle headed'. He often referred to the River Tagus as the River Thames. Wellington's subordinates were imposed on him by Whitehall and he had very little choice when it came to their employment. Spencer was accused of writing defeatist letters during one of Wellington's strategic withdrawals and lost his command. Wellington had long felt Spencer had failed to support him during the fallout over the Convention of Cintra.

[3] The retreating light infantrymen told the approaching men of the 71st, 'Seventy-First, you will come back quicker than you advance.'

This being infinitely easier said than done, the old sergeant advised me to join him in throwing it away; I agreed at once to the proposal; and we accordingly pitched it a good distance to the rear. The officer chancing to observe this instance of contempt of his authority, threatened terrible things; but to his menaces we were perfectly indifferent: for what does a man care about the chance of punishment, when the next instant may be his last?

We were preparing to load our muskets, when Cadogan called out, 'No loading; an inch of steel is worth a dozen of rounds'. Just at this time, the old sergeant was eased of his own knapsack also, in the most miraculous manner, a cannon-ball having very politely come and cut it clean off his back without doing him the slightest injury!

Our customary salute of three cheers was now given, the bagpipes struck up a warlike pibroch, and suddenly we rushed down the village street,[4] and took in an instant 100 men and 10 officers prisoners. We next crossed a small rivulet in our way, then recrossed it, skirmishing all the while, and continuing to do so, till Night, as if in compassion to foolish men, threw her sable mantle over the earth. Our regiment had thus the merit of being the first that lodged itself in the village of Fuentes de Honoro: but, as might be expected, all this honour could not be purchased without blood; two of our officers were mortally wounded, another received a severe thrust from a bayonet, and several of the privates were killed and wounded.

But I return to a more humble theme, to wit, food; two days had already elapsed since the smallest morsel had passed our lips: this would perhaps have been nothing to

---

[4] This may have been the point at which Cadogan urged his men forward with the words 'At 'em 71st! Charge 'em down the Gallowgate.' Many of the men would have known the ancient barracks at the end of the well-known street in central Glasgow. Another version gives Cadogan's words as: 'Glasgow lads; charge 'em down the Gallowgate.'

old musty knight-errants, and may be regarded as little even by the reader. We now felt the pangs of hunger to an indescribable degree. In fact, this was the case with the whole brigade we belonged to; while at the very same time, it was notorious to us all that the regiments of guards had their haversacks full of bread. These fellows were at all times kept better supplied, and more care taken of their precious persons, to keep them from any unnecessary danger or fatigue than any other regiments of the line.[5] This night, however, orders were despatched to them to deliver up as much bread as would supply the whole of us with a quarter pound of bread to each man; this was received accordingly.

Meanwhile, to prevent a surprise, the most of the men bivouacked in the street. The place being completely deserted by the inhabitants, in rummaging through the houses we procured some flour; a stray pig was also discovered. The man who was employed to kill it not being very expert at the business, the animal ran off after receiving the first stab of the bayonet; this obliged him to commence a long pursuit, making many a clumsy thrust, to our great diversion. Cadogan observing this affair, gave the awkward butcher some hearty curses, and ordered him to pin it to the ground; this he at length accomplished, and soon gave the unfortunate porker the *coup de grâce*. Sleep was at this time totally disregarded, the whole night being devoted to the baking of flour cakes.

Next morning the French commenced firing at us; we were ordered not to return it, but to go down to the edge of the river and lie under cover. Here we lay snug enough, – but, as in the fable of the boys and frogs, no sooner did we venture to put up our heads, than a shower of balls would whistle past us. This was rather a provoking predicament to be in, especially as we were all burning with thirst, and the

---

5. A feeling in the rest of the British Army that the troops of the Brigade of Guards are pampered remains to this day.

river was running close by us. One of the men, either unable to wait longer without drinking, or wishing to shew his courage, jumped hastily up and ran down to the river, filled his canteen, and came back safe and sound, contrary to our expectation; the enemy, meanwhile sending their bullets about his ears like hail. The moment our gentleman arrived, he uncorked his canteen with a triumphant air, saying, at the same time, he would now let us all drink; but lo! what was his surprise, on opening it, not to find any water within, – a bullet, having pierced the side of the canteen, had allowed every drop to escape. At this adventure, although our tongues nearly clove to our throats we could not resist the impulse of bursting out into a loud laugh – so ludicrously blank was the countenance of the water carrier, who prudently declined risking his life a second time.

A flag of truce came from the enemy, for permission to bury their dead and carry off their wounded. The request being granted, we took the opportunity of doing the same services to our own fallen comrades; in consequence of this, the remainder of the day continued quiet. To secure ourselves from any sudden surprise, we took the precaution of slightly barricading the streets with loose stones. At night I returned to the house where I had been before, and found that four sides of bacon had been discovered in my absence: this, with the addition of a bag of salt, which I had the honour of finding, formed a mess which, as the saying goes, was fit for a prince.

Next morning, the enemy being firmly determined upon obtaining possession of this village, they attacked that part of our army which was posted to the right of us. Not calculating upon thus being flanked, the whole regiment was dispersed throughout the streets and houses of the village, in expectation that the enemy must needs cross the river before coming at us. Lulled into security by this means, we were suddenly surprised by the entrance of the French on the right; the rest of them then crossed the river, and broke furiously through the barricades. Surrounded thus on all sides, and finding it useless to withstand, in our disordered state, the attack of the numerous force which was pouring into the town, we thought it no disgrace to take to our heels; I must confess our flight had something of the appearance of rabbits running from their holes. All of us succeeded in gaining the outside of the village, with the exception of half a company, who were hemmed in and taken prisoners, among which was Rae, the Paisley Methodist.

No sooner had we formed our pêle-mêle ranks in good array, than the French emerged from the village, and drew up opposite us, within musket shot. We proceeded immediately to open scattering fire upon them; the 74th and 88th[6] regiments then advanced to our relief, and instantly poured in such a terrific volley upon their ranks, that the fall of a long wall may aptly be compared to the ranks that fell; and the loss was the more important to the enemy, as those killed were chiefly grenadiers. We still continued giving and receiving a constant fire; but our ammunition running short, some of us went a little to the rear for a fresh supply. At this moment General Nightingale[7] rode up to our party and said, that as we had had plenty of fighting already, we might remain where we were. Most people will think this a very polite offer – so we thought also; but as we knew that the rest of our regiment, along with the others, were at that time preparing to charge, it was natural enough for us to be chagrined a little at not being allowed to participate in the approaching honour, whatever it might be. One of the men set us an example how to act, by running suddenly forward towards the regiment; the general, enraged at this disobedience of his orders, cried,

---

[6] The 74th (Highland) Foot and the 88th (Connaught Rangers) Foot. The 74th had lost their kilts in 1809 when they were one of six regiments the Government ordered deprived of their Highland status.

[7] Commander of the 1st Division Major General Miles Nightingall.

'Stop him!' – the words had scarcely fallen from his lips, when a cannon-ball passed so close to the fugitive as to make him wheel round by the wind of it; passing on then, it nearly grazed the head of the general's horse. I was now aroused myself by cries of *bomba*, and *courez*, from a Portugueze regiment which lay under cover near us: on looking round, I found that the warnings were addressed to me, a shell having alighted unperceived at my feet; happily, I had time to precipitate a retreat before it burst.

The heat of battle, and the confusion, enabled us to join the regiment, without further opposition being made to our wishes. We were just in time to join in the charge made upon the French with the bayonet: they were once more driven through the village. The light brigade now came to relieve us; but the fight was completely ended – chiefly through the interposition of night. This concluded the battle of Fuentes de Honoro. Our loss in the diverse engagements on the 3rd and 5th was heavy, amounting to about 200 men and 10 officers, killed, wounded, and prisoners.[8]

The author of *Don Roderick* has deigned to notice some events of the battle in the following lines: –

> And what avails thee that, for Cameron slain,
> Wild from his plaided ranks the yell was given –
> Vengeance and grief gave mountain rage the rein,

---

[8] Wellington acknowledged that the battle was one of the hardest he fought. 'If Boney had been here, we'd have been damnably licked,' he admitted. The regiment lost thirty-one men killed and 116 wounded. Two officers and around forty men were reported as captured by the French. The regiment's strength going into the battle is usually given as 320 men. Among the officers killed was Lieutenant John Graham from Dingwall, who had joined the regiment as a private. He was shot through the head as he advanced swinging his claymore, and his men pulled back under heavy fire from the French. But his soldier servant, sadly not identified in printed sources, ran forward to the lieutenant's body and opened fire on the enemy – firing at least thirty shots.

The gallant Col. Cameron[9] was wounded mortally during the desperate contest in the streets of the village called Fuentes de Honoro. He fell at the head of his native Highlanders, the 71st and the 79th, who raised a dreadful shriek of grief and rage.

Several egregious errors are contained in the above words. Either Sir Walter has been misinformed, or he has taken it upon himself a vast stretch of poetical license. He has made the 71st all 'native Highlanders,' whereas to say that there were forty or fifty of them in the whole regiment, would perhaps overrate the real number. The proportion of Lowlanders in the 79th was not so great; still there was no small quantity of them in the regiment. Sir Walter has made the 71st yell, shriek, and grieve, at the fall of a man who was an entire stranger to them. I can assure him that such demonstrations of woe were never shewn by any of us. I cannot think, either, that there would be such yelling on this occasion among the 79th, the alleged cause of it being a complete martinet in practice and disposition, and consequently not precisely the idol of the men.

Among the French prisoners taken at Fuentes, we recognised a Swiss who had deserted from us at the retreat of Corunna, and who, it appears, had gone back to the French again. One of our sergeants had the cold-blooded cruelty to go up to the colonel, and inquire if he might be allowed to shoot the man; but this brutal proposal was rejected with abhorrence.

Two days were passed over in the field of battle, without any important occurrence taking place, the hostile armies merely watching each other. We were not powerful enough

---

[9] Lieutenant Colonel Philips Cameron was the eldest son of the founder of the 79th Cameron Highlanders, Alan Cameron. Another of Alan Cameron's sons, Ewan, died in Lisbon while acting as an aide to his father. Alan Cameron's third son, Nathaniel, rose to command the second battalion of the Cameron Highlanders.

to attack the French; and they, on their part, seemed unwilling to come to blows with us. By the retiring of the enemy we were allowed to return to our old quarters at Albergeria: in performance of this journey we crossed that part of the field of Fuentes which was to the right of the village. Here we found that a good number of men had been slain on both sides; and that the Spanish peasants had stript them to the skin, instead of burying them. The sight of so many naked corpses huddled together, created feelings of disgust and humiliation: in this state it was impossible to distinguish friend from foe, Briton from Frenchman, with the exception of one body, of huge dimensions; which having a long beard, we judged to have belonged to a French pioneer.[10]

The people of Albergeria, on missing their old salesman Pacalarga from among us, made many anxious inquiries about him, but that righteous man had been wounded, and sent home to England. We were reinforced at our present cantonment by two companies from the depot: I believe if it had not been for this timely succour we should have been sent home, our regiment being so much weakened in numbers.[11]

It was about this time that the French garrison of Almeida[12] effected their escape from that fortress in such a gallant manner, although it was environed round by British and Portugueze troops: I believe the noise of the cannonading in this affair was heard in our quarters. Little or no blame could be attached to any particular part of the besieging army for this seeming negligence; fate, circumstances, or the ability of the enemy's general, may at

---

[10] The pioneers were an infantry battalion's own military engineers and jacks-of-all-trades. To this day, many pioneer units are distinguished by their beards.

[11] The strength of the 1/71st at this stage is usually given as 200 men.

[12] Commanded by General Brennier, former prisoner of the 71st.

times deceive the most wary, as one or more of these causes did in this case. However, one of those vulgar rhymes which nobody makes, but which is in the mouth of every one, was raised on this occasion: for the insertion of it I hope I may be pardoned: –

> The lions went to sleep
> The lambs out to play
> And out of Almeida
> The French marched away.

To explain this hobbling verse, it is necessary to say that the 2nd and 4th,[13] two of the implicated regiments, had for their ensigns or mottos a sphinx or lamia, and a lion: the 2nd obtained the former sign on account of the part they bore in the Egyptian expedition. It will be seen, on inspecting the foregoing distich, that by a translation as rapid as any in Ovid's Metamorphoses, the lamia is converted into a lamb.

Intelligence having arrived that a French army, under the command of Marshal Soult,[14] was advancing from Andalusia to relieve Badajoz, which was invested by

---

[13] The 4th (King's Own) Foot. The Duke of Wellington scapegoated the regiment's commanding officer Lieutenant Colonel Charles Bevan for failing to block the French escape route at the Barba de Puerco bridge. In response Bevan blew his brains out. Major General Erskine and Major General Alexander Campbell were far more to blame, but both had high-powered friends in Britain and Wellington did not dare publicly condemn them. Erskine originally intended to send only five men to guard the bridge and then, after being persuaded to employ the entire 4th Foot, scribbled down the necessary order on a piece of paper which he then put in his pocket and forgot about for more than six hours.

[14] Nicholas Jean-De-Dieu Soult was another of Napoleon's marshals who had risen from the rank of private. He had commanded the French at the Battle of Corunna in 1809. Wellington noted that Soult 'never seems to me to know how to handle troops after the battle had begun'. After his defeat in the bloody Battle of Albuera in 1811, Soult insisted

Beresford's[15] allied army of British, Portugueze, and Spaniards, our brigade, consisting of the 50th, 71st and 92nd regiments, accordingly received orders to march to their assistance. The exigency of the case demanded speed, we hastily broke up our quarters, and commenced our march southwards at the unusual hour of seven in the evening. Intense darkness coming on soon after, the whole regiment and two companies of the 92nd were separated from the rest. The whole night passed going to and fro, endeavouring to grope our way in this unknown part of the country, till day-break at length shewed that we were only six miles distant from the original place of starting. Galling as this discovery was, we hurried on; and, by dint of much sweat and toil, overtook the other part of the brigade by noon. A very short time was allowed us for the purpose of refreshing ourselves. On we went again, as quickly as possible; but the intense heat of the day, united to the fatigue, almost overpowered many a panting, way-worn straggler. Joyfully did we halt at ten o'clock in the evening, having achieved a march of twenty-seven hours almost without any intermission of repose.

For some days we continued to advance with the utmost speed, although not with the murderous rapidity of the first day's journey; and crossing the Tagus at Villa Velha, we arrived and joined the allied army on the field of Albuhera.

---

that he had won the fight but the stubborn British had not realised they were beaten. He represented France at the Coronation of Queen Victoria in 1837. Legend has it Wellington seized him by the arm at the ceremony and announced: 'I have you at last.' Soult was known to the British rank and file as 'Fighting Jack'.

[15] William Carr Beresford was no stranger to the 71st. He commanded them during the disastrous Buenos Aires campaign of 1806. In 1812 Wellington described him as 'the ablest man I have yet seen in this army'. Beresford was appointed commander of the Portuguese army with the rank of marshal. Wellington said Beresford was the best man to replace him in the event of his own death or incapacity.

To our astonishment, we learned that the bloody battle bearing that name had been fought some time previous to our arrival; thus doing away with, or rendering useless, the painful march that we had undergone.

I have no right to describe an engagement which I did not see. The tremendous slaughter on both sides, the murderous effects of the charge of the enemy's lancers on our men, and the reduction of the 3rd regiment, or Buffs, from 800 men to

The 71st spent much of the Second Peninsular Campaign as part of Major General Rowland Hill's 2nd Division.

113

40, are facts already well known. It was foolish for either British or French to claim the victory on this occasion, their loss being evidently equal, and neither party having cause to boast of any advantage. To give an idea of the mangled appearance of our troops, I may give the report of a 71st man, who was among the first that saw them. 'I saw,' said he, 'five or six regiments sitting under a tree!' It is understood that this account was rather exaggerated.

On our first entrance on the field of slaughter, a heavy, nauseous smell assailed our nostrils: this was partly caused by the immense number of dead lying buried under ground, and partly by the fleshy fuel of the fires, with which it was found necessary to expedite the extermination of those bodies which the already gorged ground was unable to take into its cold maw. The carcasses of both men and horses were thus dragged into heaps and burned: the black and scorched sites of these sacrifices were still distinctly visible to us, covered with numerous calcined bones.

We were now incorporated with General Hill's[16] little army, and in fact remained so till the end of the war. We had certainly by this means less dangerous fighting at times than Wellington's grand army; but we sustained much greater fatigue, on account of our being employed chiefly as a sort of flying army; but not a cowardly one, be it understood, – though the term flying is perhaps rather equivocal.

Leaving the remainder of Beresford's troops to join Wellington's, which had come up by this time; we made a sweep round Badajoz, and crossed the Guadiana, the grand army having invested that place; but having nothing to do with this business, we went on and encamped near Elvas. Here we were visited with one of the heaviest thunder

---

[16] Major General Sir Rowland Hill was another of Wellington's most trusted subordinates. He was one of the few British generals whom Wellington felt comfortable giving independent commands. Hill was known to his men as 'Daddy Hill'.

showers I ever recollect to have seen or felt. A few minutes after its commencement, we found ourselves lying as it were in the bed of a running stream; but such a bed not being exactly to our taste, we hastily broke down a number of branches from the neighbouring trees, with the intention of stretching our limbs upon them for the rest of the night. This contrivance succeeded pretty well, the water rushing under these little bridges, without doing us much injury. Passing through Elvas, we took up another encampment at Toro de Moro, situated within a short distance of Campo Mayor.

No immediate prospect of business in our way being in hand we were employed in constructing huts covered with broom, to keep ourselves in a more comfortable state than tents would effect, and at the same time shield off the rays of the burning summer sun. The powerful fervency of that luminary soon withering our broomy roofs, we were constrained continually to repair them, which in such weather was no small labour. Colonel Cadogan had a fine large hut built for himself, surrounded by walks and shrubbery; and the altering, mending, pruning and beautifying of this rustic palace gave continual employment to a number of the men. This sort of toil was sorely grudged by them, it being considered entirely unnecessary. One day, as Cadogan sat in his hut, the unwilling labourers began to revile and curse him amongst themselves for giving them so much trouble: little did they know that the object upon which they were expanding their wrath was close at the time. Every word of the abuse rung in Cadogan's ears, he had too much magnanimity to get into a rage, or even take notice at the time. This, I believe, was exactly the same conduct that the celebrated French general Turenne[17]

---

[17] Henri de la Tour d'Auvergne, Vicomte Turenne, was one of the most celebrated French commanders of the mid-1600s. Marshal Turenne was notorious for eavesdropping on his soldiers while on campaign. He claimed to have on more than one occasion heard his veterans insist to

pursued when placed in a similar predicament. Hearing that a draft of 350 recruits from the depot, had landed at Lisbon, and were coming up to join us, Cadogan gave us orders to build huts for them; saying at the same time, 'See that there is no grumbling among them; I heard what you said of me the other day; remember, that we are not in Glasgow barracks.' The recruits had inadvertently devoured such quantity of fruit and other garbage on the road from Lisbon, that on their arrival a severe flux attacked them, by which a good number died.

Our time of relaxation in this camp was the forenoon: we had liberty to lie in the huts during the heat of the day, and the privilege of bathing in a river which ran at no great distance from our dwellings. While laving our limbs in the crystal wave, it was no difficult task to distinguish those who had lately arrived in the country, by the superior whiteness of their skins: our own had now become nearly as brown as a fox's; in fact, the skin was such an invariable criterion, that the length of time a person had remained in the Peninsula could be told by it within a few months. On these occasions of bathing, we had often an opportunity of admiring the dexterity of the Portugueze soldiers in diving; they would remain for an astonishing length of time under water, and contrive to catch and bring up a number of fishes.

The river I have mentioned is, like most other peninsular ones, infested by numbers of water snakes and leeches: they never harmed us, however. I cannot say so much for the land serpents, at least if striking terror can be accounted a cause of complaint. An Irishman belonging to the regiment was out one day washing his shirt, and having accomplished

younger soldiers who complained about the hardships of campaign life that the marshal valued their welfare above all else. A cynic might suggest that the old soldiers, a breed noted for grumbling, might have been only too aware of the identity of the man loitering near their camp fire.

this, the process of drying it next took place: this necessary operation of course requiring some little time, Pat must needs do something to relieve his *ennui*. Espying a serpent lying close by, basking itself in the sun, he attacked it with a shillelah;[18] but the poor descendant of the old Eden deceiver was not at all disposed to encourage such striking attentions; on the contrary, it darted with the greatest fury at our hero, who, no longer willing to continue the conflict, wisely took to his heels, leaving his only shirt behind. The vindictive creature gave him chase nearly to the very camp, making many leaps, before it relinquished the pursuit. Pat was so terrified, that some of us had to go along with him, as a sort of escort, to fetch back the shirt. At another time, while we were upon the march, a serpent was discovered stretched out on the middle of the road: one of the men aimed a blow at it with the but-end of his firelock; but missing his mark, it was preparing to fly at him, when an officer drew his sword and cut it in two.

Wellington's grand army had, ere this time, been obliged to abandon the siege of Badajoz, and take refuge within the frontiers of Portugal, in consequence of the junction of the armies of Marmont[19] and Soult, the aggregate number of which was considered too powerful to contend with. The whole of Spain being thus again under the control of the enemy, measures were taken to prevent their entrance into Portugal; Wellington taking up a position on the north, or Beira side of the Tagus, while our little army received orders to do the same on the south, or Alentejo side of that river. Leaving, therefore, the camp of Toro de Moro, after a residence of six weeks there, we marched to the town of Borba.

---

[18] A stout, often gnarled, stick which was supposedly favoured as a weapon by Irishmen.

[19] Auguste Frédéric Louis de Marmont succeeded Massena as commander of the French Army of Portugal. He and Napoleon knew each other when they were both young artillery officers.

The French never having penetrated into this part of the kingdom, we found the inhabitants in as primitive and tranquil a state as if profound peace had reigned for centuries in the Peninsula. Having escaped the contamination of warlike horrors, the manners and customs of the nation were seen here in greater purity than in the north.

One day, acting as orderly to Colonel Cadogan, I found him lodged in a large genteel house. While I was dancing attendance at this place, his groom-boy, a Catholic, invited me, by way of a great favour, to go and see the lady of the house at her devotions. I went accordingly, and, on looking into a splendid room, beheld the lady kneeling before an image of the Virgin, praying with the utmost fervency, and at times offering it a cup of water. Many of the Portugueze were to be seen going about the streets at night, playing on guitars, and accompanying the music with their voices. The general term given to this custom is serenading, I understand; but I never saw them performing under the window of a favourite dulcinea, as the common acceptation of the word implies.

One of the German hussars[20] in our service met his death here by accident. He was in a sickly state, and had gone down to the side of a well to drink; in doing this it was supposed that he had fallen into it; at any rate he was found drowned: accordingly, his countrymen buried him with military honours. While they were firing over the grave, a Portugueze woman, who was looking at the ceremony, inquired seriously of us, how long the man would be in going home? or, to use her manner of expressing it, how long he would be in crossing 'La Mar'. It would appear by this, that she had an idea that Protestants consider death as only a kind of passport for their own country; – a similar opinion is held by the negroes. One of the men, well aware

---

[20] The King's German Legion had two regiments of Hussars, the 1st and 2nd, serving with the British at this time.

how useless it was to combat with bigoted prejudice, answered that the German would be 'three days in going home'.

Apparently, the zeal of the Portugueze in the common cause was not so high as might have been expected; their authorities being obliged to have recourse to the impress-ment of soldiers, in the same manner as in our enlightened country we procure seamen. It was common enough to see strings of forty men driven into the town like flocks of geese; they were all tied to each other as a security for their honour. The general costume of these recruits was knee-breeches and naked legs, along with the invariable sombrero: as for the other parts of their raiment, the genius of raggedness forbids any description but in the words 'things of shreds and patches' – the only account that comes near the truth. The scowling eyes and dusky visages of these fellows, or rather their *tout ensemble*, had a very brigand appearance. Their escort, or drivers, were generally old men, armed with rusty bayonets fastened to the ends of poles, others had guns without locks, and the like formidable weapons.

In common with other southern nations, the Portugueze have an aversion to the use of ardent spirits: although their soldiers received exactly the same allowance of every article as ourselves, yet they often came to us and exchanged their rum for biscuits. Honest enough customers for the rum were certainly found among us, – but there were some thirsty rogues also, who contrived to cheat the unsuspecting Portugueze out of a good deal of liquor; they having a polite custom of asking us to taste it out of their horns before a bargain was concluded. By this means, the mere tasters always out-numbered the buyers; and special care was taken by them not to say a word till a hearty pull was obtained from the horn; then the rum was sure to be bad or watered, and an affectation made of spitting it out with disgust. In this manner, every horn that came in their reach was pretty sure to be nearly emptied of its contents. Many of the fellows got drunk upon the *'pruevas,'* that being the name the Portugueze gave the trying of the liquor; *prueva,* or proof, having the same meaning.

We left the town of Borba, on an excessive hot morning, the scorching sun beating on our heads with prodigious force. This, in conjunction with a total want of water, caused many to hang out their parched tongues, while others fell powerless to the ground, unable to proceed. As was done to myself on a former occasion, the officers went about per-suading the fallen men to get up and move on. A strange manner of persuasion was adopted by the Highland officer who had reproved our impiety at the nunnery in such elevated terms: 'Rise up,' said he, 'I ken you are a strong man by your hough':[21] the panting object of his attention was unable to do much more than smile at this uncouth address. But to return to the subject, the whole of the men came into the halting place in small straggling parties; I was among the first to reach it, – the major part not arriving till the cool of the evening. The effects of this day's march were the putting of 300 men into the hospital, seriously injured in health: they of course belonged to different regiments of the brigade.

Next day we marched to Portalegre. The grand army had about this time made an incursion into Spain and laid siege to Ciudad Rodrigo; but they retraced their steps into Portugal again, on the approach of Marmont's army to its relief.

---

[21] An old term for thigh. It was sometimes also used to refer to sinews

Chapter Six

Having for some time escaped any dangerous service, while our other army was suffering some of its hardships, we were at length roused from our languor, by orders arriving from Wellington. We, together with some Spanish troops, were to drive General Girard's army out of Estremadura; they having been lording it over that province for some time.

Issuing forth, accordingly, from Portalegre with great alacrity on the 22nd of October, we marched with the utmost rapidity for four successive days. We entered Spain, passing through Alburquerque and Aliseda: at the latter place we were joined by the Spanish allies. The velocity of our advance soon leaving the provision waggons far behind, we were at one time obliged to make an attack on a large cabbage-field along with the starving horses and mules; however, we put the cabbages through the operation of boiling before feeding on them – and miserable cheer they were, after all.

Meanwhile, the enemy, informed of our movements, continued to retreat before us: about this time, however, he seemed to have been thrown off his guard, as we guessed, by his pace slackening by degrees, and his halt at Arroyo Molinos.[1] Due information of these circumstances reaching us, we pursued our weary way, in despite of bad roads and

---

[1] Usually rendered as Arroyo dos Molinos.

heavy rain, till we arrived within two leagues of the place. Having halted, and got some rice served out, we waited impatiently till darkness would allow us to carry our project of surprising the enemy into execution: the continuance of the wind and rain, without having permission to kindle fires, no doubt increased our wish to terminate the business as soon as possible. At two o'clock in the morning of the 28th October we started silently for the place of destination, wading amidst the muddy mountain roads in the dark till day-light broke; it was then discovered that Arroyo Molinos was in sight; and being on a rising ground, the better to escape observation, the whole army descended into a hollow. While in this situation, we saw a Spanish peasant come out of the town and commence his agricultural labours in a field; without observing that thousands of armed men were close by him.

Part of the army, under the command of General Howard,[2] was now ordered to make a circle round the town, in order to prevent the enemy's retreat; another portion, including our regiment, was instructed to advance directly on the town. Presently, the busy sound of examining flints and tying down chin-straps was heard – the certain indications of an approaching brush. All these necessary preparations being accomplished, General Hill gave the word of command, – 'Shoulder arms'. When that was done, he said, 'Move on, my lads, and *God be with you!*' Just at the time, a tremendous shower of rain came on, which, although it wet our skins, did not *damp* our courage – the secrecy of the enterprise being rather favoured than otherwise by the cloudy discharge. When we reached the outskirts of the place, a picket of French cavalry was discovered in an olive wood, squatting around some fires, with their horses tied to the trees: – they had apparently

---

[2] Major General Kenneth Alexander Howard. He was commended for his roles in the battles of Arroyo dos Molinos and Almaraz.

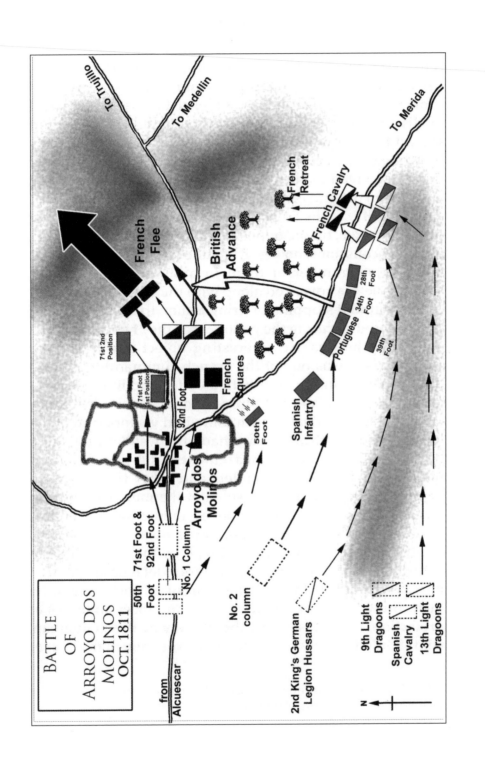

BATTLE
OF
ARROYO DOS
MOLINOS
OCT. 1811

To Trujillo

To Medellin

To Merida

French Retreat

French Cavalry

French Cavalry

French Flee

British Advance

28th Foot

34th Foot

Portuguese

39th Foot

71st 2nd Position

71st Foot 1st Position

92nd Foot

French Squares

50th Foot

Spanish Infantry

Arroyo dos Molinos

71st Foot & 92nd Foot

50th Foot

No. 1 Column

No. 2 column

2nd King's German Legion Hussars

9th Light Dragoons

Spanish Cavalry

13th Light Dragoons

from Alcuescar

N

retired to this shelter in consequence of the shower, perhaps not many minutes before our arrival – so much, as some folks would say, had Providence favoured us. Fearful of disturbing the cavalry, lest they should escape, and spread the alarm of our approach, we marched cautiously by, while they were lulled into such security that not one of them perceived us. Leaving a company to surprise them, we pushed on, and entered the town without opposition.

Early as it was, the French were at the same time marching out of the town, on the opposite side from whence we were, totally unconscious, however, of our presence; but there was still a good number of them in and about the houses. Meanwhile, we advanced along with the 92nd, according to orders, without stopping or firing a shot; the 50th following close behind, securing the prisoners as they ran distractedly out of the houses. An interesting object now drew our attention, – it was one of the French commanders, Prince d'Aremberg,[3] running out with a coffee cup in his hand, – alarm and astonishment strongly depicted on his countenance, at the arrival of such uninvited visitors, and at the joyous shouts with which we made the welkin[4] ring. Little time was allowed for his amazement to subside: scarce an instant elapsed till the epaulets and other frippery were plucked from his person by some of the men. He was also rather roughly treated, being shoved about from side to side, in order to compel him to join in the noisy cheering: this request was at length complied with by the poor man, but with great reluctance, and endeavours to let it be known that he was a 'principe'. To save himself from further ill usage, he then threw himself into the arms of an officer, in hopes of protection, – but was rudely thrust away by this gentleman, who should have known better: however, men in the heat of

---

[3] The 7th Duke of Arenberg, Prosper Louis, and the colonel of the Belgian Chevau-Légers d'Arenberg.
[4] The sky or heavens.

a confusion such as this, may be hurried into actions which they will blush for at a cooler moment.

Continuing our course through the town, we met the body of French cavalry direct in the teeth, who had been dislodged from the wood at the first outset of the affair; they had fled by a circuitous route, and thus came unexpectedly upon us. Seeing no other means of escape but that of forcing through us, they charged with the fury of despair: unfortunately, our muskets were in such a state, on account of the late rains, that few or none of them would give fire. This encouraged the horsemen, they being now intermixed with us, hewing and cutting on all sides; some of them penetrated to the place where Colonel Cadogan was: a blow aimed at him divided his cap in two, but, happily, the sword glanced off without doing any real injury.[5] The Marquess of Tweeddale,[6] and a Major Churchill, perceiving the colonel's imminent danger, immediately rode up and cut down the assailant, at the same time completely dispersing the others.

We had ere this betaken ourselves to the trusty bayonet; one of the men had driven his with such force into the body of a horse, that the animal, writhing with pain, made a sudden jerk, and ran off a good distance, with both musket and bayonet sticking in its side, the rider being unable to stop its furious course: the owner of the arms soon afterwards recovered them. At length the horsemen were overcome by numbers, and either all killed or taken prisoners: their bravery was the admiration of the men,

---

[5] The Frenchman wielding the sword was the colonel of the 34th Regiment rather than a cavalryman and was galloping through the village to join his men when he encountered Cadogan. The French colonel was disarmed and captured rather than killed as the author asserts.

[6] George Hay, 8th Marquis of Tweedale, and an aide-de-camp to the Duke of Wellington between 1807 and 1813. Hay later became a field marshal and his daughter Elizabeth married Wellington's son Arthur and became the 2nd Duchess of Wellington.

although it was to our cost, several of our soldiers being slain or wounded. The whole time the contest was going on, the Spanish inhabitants were looking on, and shouting 'success to the red coats' in their own language.

This last obstacle surmounted, we passed on to the end of the town without further obstruction; here the remainder of the enemy were drawn up in a wavering state, uncertain whether to fight or fly; this suspense was soon settled by our opening on them a destructive fire, while the Portugueze artillery commenced playing upon their ranks with appalling havoc; panic overpowered them, and suddenly some of the French flung down their arms and fled; the rest, keeping up as much appearance of order as their situation would admit, immediately commenced a precipitate retreat, but this was promptly baulked by the appearance of General Howard's troops in their path: the enemy were thus entirely enclosed on all sides; terror and surprise caused every restraint to be abandoned, and irretrievable confusion took place amongst them: 'save himself who can', was the order of the day, and happy was he who gained the summit of the neighbouring hills. Others took flight along the Road; but on all sides they were hotly pursued by the Spanish cavalry and infantry, along with such of the British and Portugueze as were not yet exhausted with fatigue.

Such a complete victory as this seldom occurs, nearly the one half of the enemy's army being taken prisoners, amounting to little short of 2,000 men, including the Prince d'Aremberg, General Brun, and many other officers;[7] the rest of the trophies were, the whole of the enemy's artillery,

---

[7] The number of French troops captured was between 1,300 and 1,500. A further 1,000 were believed to have been killed or wounded. The troops were reckoned to be amongst the best in the French army. The high-ranking officers were escorted to Lisbon by the 71st's Captain Robert Barclay. The colours of the French 40th Regiment hung in the officers' mess of the 71st for many years. But oddly only the 34th (Cumberland) Foot received the battle honour 'Arroyo-dos-Molinos'.

magazines of corn, baggage, and even some money which had been forced from the Spaniards under the name of a contribution.

The battle of Arroyo Molinos, small as it was, comparatively speaking, may be said to have been the first decided advantage the British obtained in this war; it was the first instance, at any rate, in which they had acted on the offensive, and its results were splendid, unlike those of our former engagements.

Leaving Molinos, we advanced to Merida, and afterwards returned to Portalegre. In December following, intelligence arrived that a French army under Dombrowski[8] was ravaging Estremadura, our army received orders to enter that province, in order to chastise or expel the invaders. Having marched so far on our way, we came unexpectedly on a party of 300 French busily employed cooking; these men no sooner descried us, than they hastily started up, formed a square with great presence of mind, and commenced a retreat. Our cavalry taking the lead, pursued, and made several ineffectual attempts to break them; the gallant little band repulsing the horsemen with great slaughter at every charge. The celerity of the enemy's progress prevented our cannon from making any serious impression, one ball alone taking effect, killing three men and wounding two others. At one time a company of us were mounted behind the horsemen, with the intention of being carried speedily forward, and set down close by the French, in order to try the effect of infantry, but this scheme was not carried into execution; for, to their honour be it said, the enemy succeeded in reaching Merida in safety, after having kept our whole army at bay for the greater part of a day. During the pursuit, immense flocks of carrion crows hovered over us in seeming expectation of a battle; animal

---

[8] Polish patriot Jan Henryk Dombrowski organised a Polish Legion in 1795–6 to fight for the French.

instinct teaching them that the abundance of food is to them the result of such an event.

Dombrowski flying precipitately on our approach, we passed through Merida and advanced as far as Villa Franca, scaring and putting to flight another little array under Drouet.[9] Then wheeling about, we returned to Portalegre; passing, by the way, the bodies or rather skeletons of three Frenchmen who had been slain about eight days before. An anatomist could not have scraped the flesh cleaner off a body than the crows had done off those of these men; the bones looked as if they had been boiled or bleached white. Although the prompt destruction of putrid carcasses be beneficial to the health of the living, yet we hate the destroyer, or, in more common words, 'we like the treason but detest the traitor': the dingy birds were therefore held in abhorrence ever after.

Our late expedition having cut off the communication of Soult and Marmont's armies, Wellington's army was enabled to lay siege to Ciudad Rodrigo with the greater security. In the beginning of the year 1812 we moved northward to Castella Branca, and met there a number of French prisoners coming from Ciudad Rodrigo;[10] that important fortress having been stormed and captured by our grand army. Two companies of our regiment were detached to Lisbon as an escort to the prisoners; meanwhile the army returned, for the last time, to Portalegre.

On the news of Wellington having invested Badajoz reaching us, we marched towards that place, passing through Alburquerque and crossing Guadiana; by which time we found ourselves in the midst of the besieging army, witnesses and listeners to the terrible fire kept up between

---

[9] Jean-Baptiste Drouet, Count d'Erlon, was another former ranker who commanded the Army of Portugal.

[10] Ciudad Rodrigo was captured on 9 January 1812 at the cost of over 1,000 casualties.

them and the French garrison. Parting from the grand army on the evening of the same day, we advanced as far as Don Bonito, our orders being to cover its operations. Although sixty miles distant from Badajoz, we still could hear the roar of the artillery employed in the siege, particularly in the mornings or other calm intervals: perhaps the river Guadiana contributed to carry the sound, that stream running by our quarters, and washing the walls of Badajoz at the same time. After sojourning in Don Bonito for a week, we fell back on Merida and blew up a bridge there, in order to stop the progress of Soult's army, which was advancing with the intention of relieving Badajoz. We continued to retire till the flashes of the guns and musketry engaged in the siege were visible. Soon after this we received news of the surrender of Badajoz; this event was celebrated among us with the powerful aid of extra rum. Colonel Cadogan stood in front of the regiment, and set an example by drinking 'Success to the British arms' or something to that import; thus, for the first time, Cadogan officiated as a flugleman[11] to his own men.

The successful issue of two sieges, and the subsequent retreat of the enemy's armies, emboldened Wellington to form another project, – this was to destroy the bridge of Almaraz,[12] it being the common thoroughfare between the north and south of Spain, and thereby considered a post of the greatest consequence. On account of our army having escaped the dangers of Rodrigo and Badajoz, it was thought fit to intrust us with the execution of the scheme. Proceeding therefore, to Almadralego, where a draft from Britain joined

---

[11] Fugleman is a German military term meaning a soldier stationed on the wing of a unit to act as a guide. In this context it means ring-leader or cheer-leader.

[12] The forts at Alamaraz protected a pontoon bridge across the Tagus, the destruction of which would prevent the French under Marshal Soult joining the army of Marshal Marmont for an attack on Wellington.

us, we passed through Merida, and marched to Truxillo where six companies of the men were quartered in Pizzaro's[13] house: many changes have taken place to this dwelling; this was another; General Hope and his staff had been lodged in it when we were here in 1808.

Still pursuing our way towards Almaraz, we at one time halted, and were exercised in the duties of escalade, this business being entirely new to us: scaling ladders were placed on each side of the parapets of a bridge, the feet of the ladders resting on the dry bed of the rivulet; whoever then ran up the one side and down on the other in the nimblest manner, was considered the most meritorious. Part of the army was now detached to attack the castle of Mirabete, a fortified place, perched on an exceeding high mountain, and commanding a pass near Almaraz. Moving on, then, after our odd, but necessary preliminary instructions in storming, we marched a whole night, in hopes of surprising the enemy betimes; but daylight shewing that the place of destination was still at too great a distance for such an attempt, it was thought requisite, from the state of the roads, to leave the artillery, and ascend a mountainous road; where, as the attack was deferred till the following morning, we were allowed to repose ourselves till night. In a few minutes nearly the whole brigade lay fast asleep, but a sudden cry of 'stand to your arms!' made every one start on his feet: on all sides, the noise of fixing bayonets, and other warlike preparations, was heard; such words never being uttered except in cases of imminent danger. It was soon discovered, however, that the alarm had proceeded from one of the men, in his dream. Just as Mercutio says; –

---

[13] Trujillo, as it is usually spelled now, was the birthplace of the four Pizzaro brothers, Hernando, Francisco, Juan and Gonzalo, who all played a role in the conquest of Peru by the Spanish.

And then dreams of cutting foreign throats,
Of breaches, ambuscadoes, Spanish blades.[14]

Similar occurrences are not uncommon among military men: I have seen 20,000 men extended on the ground, to all appearance buried in sleep, yet at the slightest alarm or noise of any kind, every one of this large body of men would start up simultaneously, and prepare for action. This was done the more readily if the enemy was in the neighbourhood. In fact, the mind on such occasions is in something of the same state as that of the traveller who has to get up from his couch at a fixed time, and who is consequently in terror of oversleeping himself.

Night now approaching, and the object of our mission being still unperformed, not to speak of a tiresome tramp besides, we marched, or rather clambered off, a company of us carrying a quantity of broom to burn the bridge, and two of the best swimmers in the regiment were in readiness to bring the bridge back, if the enemy attempted to set it adrift; however, these plans were not carried into effect, for divers reasons. The difficulties of picking our steps through the mountains were much increased by the inky darkness of the night; no paths could be found save those made by the goatherds, these men being in reality the only human beings who disturbed the solitude of these wilds. Their roads, it may be judged, therefore, were not of an unmeasurable breadth; so did we find, as sometimes only one man could pass them at a time: but it is needless to drag the reader along the whole way; it is sufficient to say, that, after having several marvellous escapes from falling over precipices, we descended into a valley on the morning of the 19th of May, and came in sight of the bridge, with all its forts and fortifications.

---

[14] A quote from William Shakespeare's *Romeo and Juliet.*

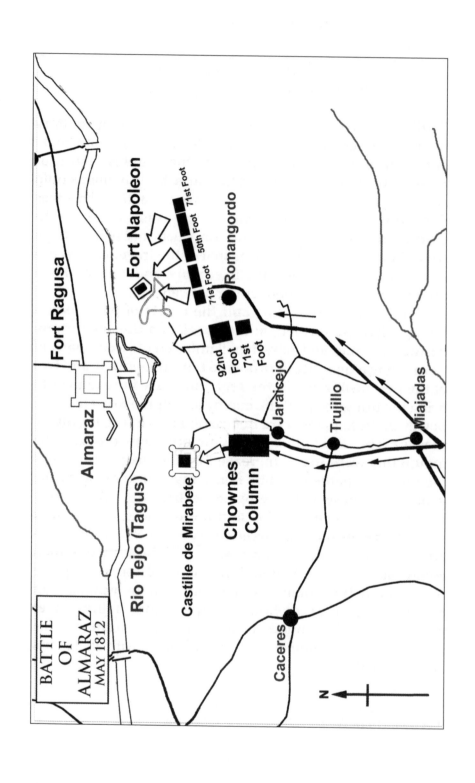

BATTLE OF ALMARAZ MAY 1812

Fort Ragusa

Fort Napoleon

Almaraz

Rio Tejo (Tagus)

Romangordo

71st Foot

50th Foot

71st Foot

71st Foot

92nd Foot

71st Foot

Jaraicejo

Trujillo

Miajadas

Castille de Mirabete

Chownes Column

Caceres

N

The enemy being fully apprised of our approach, we were saluted instantly with some cannon-balls from their nearest battery. As time is precious on such occasions, it was thought expedient to employ only the 50th[15] regiment and a wing of ours, as the storming party. They accordingly advanced to the assault, and in a short time placed their ladders against the walls of Fort Napoleon; the remainder of us, along with the 92nd, kept stationary, about a hundred yards from the walls, ready to give support if required. Our comrades were now to be seen mounting the ladders, regardless of the heavy fire which the enemy poured down upon them; the fire was returned from some at the foot of the walls, yet a number of the men were shot or thrust off the ladders with bayonets before an entrance was effected, which was done at length, every opposition being borne down, a 71st man entering the place first of all, – a thing very gratifying to us, of course. Almost at the very instant Fort Napoleon was taken possession of, the enemy began to pour a cannonade into it from Fort Ragusa, on the opposite side of the river Tagus: this precipitation gained them nothing, as a body of their own countrymen were rushing out at the gate, endeavouring to escape the bayonets of our men; they were nearly swept off to a man by this ill-timed fire. The guns of Fort Napoleon were now turned against Ragusa, which in a short time compelled the garrison to consult their safety in flight: and the whole achievement of storming and carrying the fortifications of Almaraz was accomplished in the short space of fifteen minutes.

Liberty was now given to pile arms; and we spectators set off full speed towards the fort, for the purpose of coming in for a share of whatever booty was going. Some stingy officers attempted to throw obstructions in the way, but

---

[15] The 50th was commanded at the time by Lieutenant Colonel Charles Stewart, who had served as a captain in the 71st in India in the early 1790s.

General Hill commanded them to desist, saying, that 'we had wrought hard enough for any thing which might be obtained'. Reaching the desired haven, we found that an interesting scene of noise and confusion was taking place since the din of war had ended: numbers of tame goats were running about on all sides, flying from the men, who were eagerly pursuing them with no friendly intent. It seems that almost every one of the French garrison had been possessed of a goat or two, either for pets or for their milk, or perhaps for both purposes. Immense magazines of provisions and spirits were also laid open to our attacks, – they consisted of rice, biscuits, hams, brandy, &c.: the filling of haversacks and canteens gave employment for some time, in consequence of this God-send. But a 50th man was the most successful of any, he coming out of some secret place or other with his cap filled with gold doublons:[16] each of these coins is equivalent to 3*l* 7*s*. sterling; it may be judged, therefore, that a capful of them would constitute a pretty round sum. A 71st man had the good fortune to find a colour belonging to the corps *étranger*;[17] for, to be candid, I must say, that he had not an opportunity of taking it by force of arms, – but the difference of the honour is merely ideal; for what, in reality, is the honour of a stained rag?

Having no intention of keeping possession of our conquest, our mission being only to destroy, we set about dismantling the works with great alacrity: while some part of Fort Ragusa was undergoing this operation by blasting, we could perceive some of the men running as usual from where an explosion was to take place; it went off soon after, carrying at the same time a human being up into the air. It was discovered that the unfortunate person was Lieutenant Thiele, a German engineer officer, in our service; he had

---

[16] Also spelled dubloon or doubloon.
[17] The flag belonged to the 4th Battalion of the Corps Êtranger. It was sent to the Duke of Wellington.

imprudently gone back to the fatal spot, under the idea that the fuse had gone out, but the melancholy sequel shows that he had been mistaken.

Almaraz being at length rendered incapable of defence, and its bridge of boats annihilated, the men abandoned themselves to joy: the whole of the following night was spent in feasting, drinking, and singing; every remembrance of their fallen comrades being drowned in present enjoyment. Next morning we marched off, so heavily laden with spoil that, at one time, the Colonel threatened to cut off our haversacks, in order to make swifter travellers. After halting in our former encampment in the mountains, we returned to Truxillo; here the inhabitants received us with great rejoicings, on account of our late successes: by the by, I may mention here, that the Almaraz exploit had (in our own opinion, at least) closed the balance of valour with the heroes of Rodrigo and Badajoz, although on a smaller scale.[18]

To gratify the people and us, at this time of general conviviality, the authorities of Truxillo ordered a bull-fight to be performed in the Plaça,[19] or public square. I suspect this fight was conducted on a more humble plan than is done on some occasions; no armed horse or foot attacked the bull in this instance, which is the usual manner, according to book accounts. The animal was merely fastened by a long rope to a ring, in the middle of the square; this gave him a good deal of scope: the Spaniards then ran up and shook cloths or handkerchiefs in his face, till he was rendered furious: that was the time of the cream of the sport, as it seemed, for at the moment the bull was stooping to gore its tormentor, the latter contrived, with admirable agility, to escape, to the infinite delight and edification of the spectators. From the

---

[18] The 71st lost nine men killed and thirty-four wounded in the fighting at Almaraz. A total of thirty-six non-commissioned officers and men were recognised in battalion orders for conspicuous bravery.

[19] More usually rendered in English as Plaza.

skill of the Spaniards at such exercises, I believe the entertainment would have passed over without bloodshed had not one of the British, a 60th rifleman, foolishly mixed among the combatants; but, of course, being far inferior to them in adroitness, he was overtaken by the ferocious beast, and tossed with dreadful violence into the air. The hapless man was taken up in a shocking condition; he expired soon after.

We continued our march to Merida, where a prisoner, the French governor of Almaraz, died of his wounds; he was buried with every military honour due to his rank. Leaving this place, we arrived at Almandralego. Here a new chaplain was appointed to preach to the brigade: instead of laying his books only on the drum-head, he suddenly jumped himself, with all the agility of a mountebank, on the top of that noisy instrument; this action naturally drew a deafening laugh from the soldiery, they expecting every instant to see the chaplain make his exit through the skin: he had almost commenced an oration, when Colonel Stewart, of the 50th, warned him of the mistake.

Our army now received orders to make a diversion in the south, while Wellington was moving northward to Salamanca. Leaving Almandralego, therefore, we marched for some time, passing through the towns of Zafra and Llerana: the enemy's flying parties, who infested Estremadura, were driven before us in all directions, our advanced parties of cavalry being engaged every day with them. We halted at length, on the outskirts of Balranga on account of doubts existing that the enemy were in that place. In the course of the night, the whole camp was thrown into an uproar, a crashing and tumbling of the piled arms were heard, accompanied by a furious rushing sound: the idea that the French cavalry had broken in upon us was taken for granted; but the alarm was instantaneously quashed, by a discovery that the cause of it arose from one poor stray bullock, which had probably escaped from the knife of the butcher. Next day we marched into the town, where we took up our quarters. Provisions had not been abundant of late; the sight of a large flock of sheep, therefore, awakened every appetite; but how to get at them was the question: no reasonable pretext for so doing being at hand, some bright genius or other raised a cry that they were 'French sheep'. This was enough; for with one accord, the whole brigade rushed upon the flock, and seized every one of them, the poor Spanish shepherds standing all the while mute with astonishment at such a wanton act of superior power. I know not whether these men were remunerated for their loss or not: at any rate, we were more successful in this exploit than Don Quixote[20] was in his memorable attack of the fleecy warriors.

Balranga, the utmost limit of our southern excursions, is situated on the confines of Andalusia, about twenty leagues from Cadiz, and not far from the Mediterranean: the celebrated range of mountains called Sierra Morena is close by the town. This Sierra is, I believe, the supposed scene of some of Don Quixote's pranks. Wheeling about, we returned to Zafra.

During our stay at this place a bull-fight took place, which a second time proved disastrous to my countrymen. Just as some pickets were going from the town to the camp, the bull appeared on its way to the Plaça; some Spaniards led him along with a rope, but no sooner did he observe our men, than a furious charge was made upon them; they not being prepared to encounter such an uncouth foe, prudently took refuge in the surrounding houses and stairs: one un-fortunate man, however, was ripped up along the whole back, by a single blow, just at the moment he was stooping to enter a door. The grisly savage then continued his course up a street, where the band was playing before Colonel Cadogan's door, seated at the same time round a large table. The musicians being well aware of their inferiority to

---

[20] The fictional and foolish knight created by the Spanish satirist Cervantes in a book published in 1605.

Orpheus,[21] in point of ability to tame brutes, also fled in every direction; the beast now employed himself in smashing the table and overturning the forms; in this havoc, the music-books were all torn and scattered about, neither did the band-master's costly clarionet escape the general destruction. At length, the sentinel at the colonel's door took courage, and made a thrust at the bull with a fixed bayonet, which merely glanced off his thick scull, without doing much damage, although the bayonet was bent. This attack served, however, to startle him, and he set off at full speed towards a narrow street, where the regimental guard was loitering about: some of the men escaped into the guard-house, others got behind a bullock-car; but one foolhardy Irishman stood rooted to the spot, in spite of his comrades' entreaties to save himself. This man had been at all times of a cross and perverse disposition, doing every thing in the true spirit of contradiction. Unhappily, he supported his character in this instance, and thereby drew upon himself the punishment of vain temerity: the bull coming up, mangled him in a dreadful manner; this and the former victim died in great agony. The conductors of the bull had kept hold of the rope the whole time; but finding it impossible to restrain his impetuosity, they still held on, and ran as he ran: he was at length forced into the Plaça, and the fight took place, notwithstanding the recent tragical events.

From Zafra we marched to Villa Franca; it was about this time that the news of Wellington's signal victory of Salamanca reached us: liquor was served out, and the colonel acted as flugleman again, in consequence of the joyful event. The 50th regiment having all been seized with sore eyes; they were sent to a village in the neighbouring mountains, for the benefit of better air, and to prevent the rest of the brigade from being infected: this circumstance

---

[21] A figure from Greek mythology reputed to be able to charm all living things with his music.

138

made our duty harder than usual, until the invalids recovered. We now set off to Don Bonito, and reached it after a circuitous march of five days.

In these marches through Estremadura, the weather was insufferably hot: scarcely a breath of air was stirring, and the long drought had formed such quantities of dust on the roads, that the tread of so many feet raised it about us in clouds, making every one like a miller with the whiteness. When the smallest symptoms of a passing breeze appeared, every tongue was hung out, for the purpose of obtaining a momentary refreshing coolness. Sometimes a good deal of misery was avoided by travelling at night: on such occasions we went along very pleasantly, a number of the men singing their best songs, others joining in the chorusses. While lying encamped after, a long march, it was surprising, to see with what vivacity the men started up to pursue the hares which sometimes unwarily entered the camp; never did one escape when the whole brigade joined in the chase uttering loud yells, – the noise striking it powerless with terror.

It being the fruit season at our present residence, Don Bonito, many nocturnal parties were formed by the men, for the purpose of secretly pillaging the neighbouring gardens: immense loads of fruit (chiefly figs) were brought in upon spread greatcoats; shirts, formed into temporary bags, were also used for the same laudable purpose. An old Spaniard made a remark, that the French had reaped his harvest last year, – we had done it this, – but that he would have it to himself next year. This random prophecy proved eventually true, as the belligerent powers did not make this part of the country the theatre of war again.

Chapter Seven

Lord Wellington's army having entered Madrid after the battle of Salamanca,[1] we set off in the direction of the metropolis, as I presumed for the purpose of co-operating with them. We crossed the Guadiana, and traversed our old road again, passing through Truxillo to Almaraz. At the latter place, some of the men went down to the ruins of Fort Napoleon, to examine the scene of their former exploit. They found several of our men's bodies, which had been but partially covered with earth: the rain had washed it off, and exposed the grinning skeletons to view: even in this state, a well-known sergeant was discovered amongst them, by a particular mark on his coat. The visitors took care to hide them better from the air, and came away affected with the gloomy silence of the place, which had been so very different only a few months before.

Crossing the Tagus here on pontoons, we marched to Talavera: here I went, according to my usual custom, to look for the house I had lodged in the first time we were in the country but after a long search, I found the whole street

---

[1] The French under Marshal Marmont lost about 7,000 killed and wounded at the Battle of Salamanca and an equal number of men captured. Wellington lost around 4,750 men.

where it had been situated was reduced to a heap of ruins, – such a woful change had four years of this cursed war produced. Leaving this dilapidated town, we passed our way through a beautiful country: ripe grapes hung temptingly within our reach on both sides of the road; every finger was stretched to have a pull at them; but Colonel Cadogan keeping a strict look-out for the benefit of the unfortunate proprietors, little could be obtained in day-light, although this abstinence was abundantly made up for at night. It is difficult to restrain men in such cases: the work of a few is nothing in comparison; but the labour of our multitudes was sufficient to destroy a whole vintage. Any one that was detected in the act was punished, by being obliged to carry the bass-drum for a certain distance.

At length we approached the famous city of Toledo, and were welcomed every where with joyful acclamations. A number of nuns turned out of a convent, shaking hand-kerchiefs and shouting many *vivas* to us, while we were marching by; the town bells were set a-ringing, and an illumination ordered to be prepared, to celebrate our arrival. Such unequivocal demonstrations of real joy arose from the cheerful aspect of Spanish affairs at that time; the capital being recovered, and the whole kingdom nearly rescued from French thraldom.

I walked through the town to view the illuminations, which, upon the whole, was much like what is seen in our own country, with the exception of a tall spire, which was hung from top to bottom with variegated lamps: this certainly had a very brilliant effect. We left this interesting scene, and advanced to Aranjuez, – a place remarkable for containing a splendid palace belonging to the Spanish royal family, situated amidst rich gardens, extensive parks, and noble avenues of trees, the river Tagus running through the centre of the grounds. But the description of such enchant-ing scenery must be left to the pens of a Scott or a Radcliffe; I own my incompetency to the task with the utmost humility.

During our stay here, many of our officers visited Madrid, to enjoy the festivities which had been going on there ever since the entrance of the British.

From Aranjuez we moved to Ponte Duino, farther up the Tagus. One day, while a number of men were bathing in the river, a party of French cavalry came in sight. This naturally caused every one to make the best of his way towards the shore, with the exception of a droll fellow, who stood for some time slapping a nameless part in derision of the Frenchmen. On seeing this, some of them unloosed their carbines and fired a shot or two at our hero, who then thought proper to fly. Some of the 60th riflemen turned out from their quarters on hearing the noise; and by discharging a few shots, soon made the horsemen scamper out of sight.

At Ponte Duino I first had an opportunity of witnessing the mode of feeding among the Spanish soldiery. In this respect it must be granted that they were much more military than ourselves; – for example, I saw a party of them drawn up in the form of a circle, with a kettle of soup in the centre; one man at a time advanced to the object of attack, and after having swallowed a single spoonful of the mess, he returned to his place and resumed a stiff, erect posture; the next did the same, and so on in rotation till the whole of the soup disappeared.

Suddenly we were aroused by the near approach of 70,000 French, consisting of the armies of Soult and Suchet,[2] from Andalusia and Valencia: their late reverses in the north had caused this hostile movement. Every idea of stopping the progress of such a formidable host being given up, we left our present station at night-fall, for the purpose of joining Wellington, who had now relinquished the siege of Burgos.

---

[2] Marshal Louis Gabriel Suchet began his military career in 1792 as a volunteer cavalryman in the National Guard. Napoleon said, 'If I had two more generals like him to lead my troops in Spain the war would be over.'

143

We continued to push on with little intermission till the following night, when, as we were trudging along a bridge, very tired, and half asleep, a sort of panic arose; some fixing their bayonets, others jumping upon the parapet walls, either to see or escape the expected danger. However, as nothing appeared, we quietly encamped, laughing at the false alarm, which, after all, had arisen from one of the men thinking he had seen a horse fly by him like a flash of lightning!

Previous to marching again, we were ordered to empty our haversacks of a quantity of potatoes, which had come into our possession – no matter how. Leaving many piled heaps of these roots on the ground, we journeyed for two days, and arrived at Madrid, not in it, – for a short halt only was made at the end of a bridge, until the British garrison marched out of the city and joined us. We then moved off altogether, abandoning the capital to the enemy. Thus, although it was the second time I had been close to Madrid, yet fate seemed to have decreed that I should never enter it: no great matter, some will say; perhaps so.

The Escurial was the end of our next stage: alterations had taken place here, too, since my first visit. A strong wall was built across the principal street, filled with loop-holes. This work had been projected by Joseph Buonaparte,[3] to defend himself from the Guerillas, who had extended their incursions to the palace gates. It will, perhaps, serve to give an idea of the unwieldy size of this mighty structure, the palace, – to say what was actually done; to wit, that our whole division of 20,000 men lay for a night in its lobbies or

---

[3] Joseph Bonaparte was Napoleon's elder brother and had been made King of Spain, as José I, in 1808. He began life as Guiseppe Buonaparte. His brother finally allowed him to abdicate after the British victory at Vitoria in 1813 and lived in exile in the United States between 1817 and 1832. He financed his life in the United States by selling the Spanish Crown Jewels.

passages. The rooms were locked up, and the priests had fled to some more congenial soil, as we supposed.

From the Escurial we crossed the same pass in the mountains which we had crossed four years before; and passing afterwards through Alva de Tormas, the main body of Wellington's army joined us. Nigh to the latter place, immense heaps of human and horse bones lay whitening in the air: the owners of them had been slain in the pursuit, after the battle of Salamanca. The enemy having now concentrated the whole of their forces in Spain, for the avowed purpose of driving the British back to Portugal again, Lord Wellington still continued encamped in the vicinity of Alva de Tormas, but detached our brigade into that town to defend it as long as possible. We found the walls of the place old and dilapidated: however, preparations for a vigorous resistance were made, – 300 men were posted in an old castle, and the streets barricaded with loose stone dikes.

Next day the French army appeared advancing directly upon the town: we commenced skirmishing with their advanced parties; but orders being given to refrain from acting on the offensive, we lay close behind the entrenchments, such as they were. Meanwhile the enemy opened up a heavy fire from twenty pieces of cannon, which, by our precautions for personal safety, only wrought destruction among the deserted houses. A man at my side had a narrow escape – he saw a cannon-ball coming towards him but had the presence of mind to draw back; while doing so, the ball grazed his forehead, carried off some skin, and only rendered the place of a blackish red colour. Colonel Cadogan soon afterwards saw the man, and remarked that he must have had a d—d hard skull. The enemy continued to batter away the whole day without intermission, or receiving a single answering shot from us, we being only ready to repel in case of their coming to close quarters. While in this situation, one of the men having picked up some unknown sort of root, and eat of it, along with another man, they both became stupified, and even furious, striking every person near them, and playing the most antic tricks; upon which an officer, under the idea that they were drunk, ordered them to be confined. This was effected with no small difficulty, a stout resistance of kicking and sprawling being made on their part.

On the following morning, orders came from Wellington that we should abandon the post, the enemy having crossed the river unperceived the preceding evening; and they would have probably surrounded us had we not retired, leaving 300 Spaniards in the castle. After blowing up a bridge in the course of the retreat, we joined the grand army in safety. It was afterwards reported, that these Spaniards had held their station courageously for seven days before surrendering.

The whole army now moved off, taking its way by a road leading through an immense forest: a pretty long march brought us to its edge. We then found ourselves on the field of Salamanca, where we formed immediately on the ridge which had been the position of the French on that bloody occasion. The ground every where betrayed symptoms of the late death-game, by the legs and arms which stuck out in full view: these were also convincing proofs of the manifold toils of the military sextons. Our ruminations were soon cut short by the enemy emerging from the wood, – instantly, therefore, a company of the 60th rifle corps were detached to skirmish with them; but scarcely had they left us, when a body of French cavalry were seen advancing at a gallop for the purpose of charging. The cavalry perhaps would have made short work with the riflemen, if our artillerymen had not, by a well-timed discharge, compelled them to wheel round and return as quick as they came. I observed one fellow in particular: he was lifted up from his saddle by a cannon-ball, and fell to the ground seemingly unhurt; for the next instant he rose and ran off: his horse also took to flight, but in a different direction.

The cannon being placed in a position admirably adapted for committing mischief, they were opened upon the enemy's column with terrible effect: at every discharge, a space was seen in their ranks which would admit a waggon! Lord Wellington and his staff remained for some time stationary in front of our regiment: as several of them had telescopes, a more particular estimation of the enemy's loss could thus be obtained at almost every shot. Some one of those spectators who had glasses encouraged the artillery, by crying out, – 'That is a good one!' The enemy at length sheltered themselves in the wood, thinking, probably, that affairs were taking a too tragical turn: an aide-de-camp, in my hearing, said that their loss could not be less than 1,000; – this is a round number, to be sure, but in my opinion not far from the truth. Strange it is, however, that the minds of men have been so perverted as to exult according to the number of their slain opponents!

We entered the wood while it was getting dark, and were obliged to stretch ourselves on the ground supper-less, – water, that requisite for cooking, not being at hand. Next morning the whole army formed upon the same ground as before: the French army was also drawn up in formidable array. Every appearance of a bloody battle was in prospect; but on the enemy's attempting to turn our right, Lord Wellington gave the order to retreat in the direction of Portugal. Thus had the Spanish campaign come to nought again.

Our regiment was left by itself on a height, for the purpose of amusing the enemy while the British army was filing off. We stood a full hour shivering in a storm of rain, till the last of them had passed by, when a general officer rode back from the rear, and cried to Cadogan, – 'If you do not move from that station, your men will be prisoners in less than ten minutes'. We waited not for a second invitation, but set off through some ploughed fields, which, as usual, clogged our feet, – the heavy rain still continuing, and reducing the earth to a pulp. For a further precaution against the pursuers, we formed a square: one of the companies performing its part awkwardly in this evolution, the colonel threatened to leave the men behind to the enemy: such a menace was perhaps less terrific than he imagined. By the time we reached the road, the rain had increased to such a degree that the water was up to our knees. In the midst of this interesting scene, a number of soldiers' wives and children, mounted on asses, finding it impossible to keep up with us, began a concert of cries and tears; but as no assistance could be afforded, they fell into the enemy's hands.

All the while, our cavalry and the enemy's kept firing at each other; – being muffled up in cloaks, they loaded their carbines under these coverings in perfect security from the rain: the skirmishing would have had a very picturesque appearance to an unconcerned spectator. We were nearly out of breath when a junction was effected with the rest of the brigade, – a very hasty trot having been resorted to latterly. Colonel Stewart called to Cadogan, that he had never expected to see us again. I believe, in this instance, we kept the old precept well in mind; to wit, 'a good pair of heels is worth two pair of hands'.

That evening, bivouacking again in the woods, we were startled by the noise of musketry in several directions: after all, it turned out that an immense drove of hogs had occasioned this alarm; they had probably been placed in the forest for the sake of security; but that they no longer found, few escaping from the ball and the bayonet. This unexpected supply created a redundancy of food and every belly and haversack was filled. Next night, while reposing our limbs, and cooking, after a long day's march, a large body of French cavalry was observed advancing towards us: this was particularly provoking, we being obliged to empty our kettles and stand to arms: some cannon were brought to the edge of the wood, and preparation made to allow our cavalry to act at a fit opportunity. The enemy having approached to the desired distance, the artillery gave them a warm salute, and a company of the 28th,[4] who were rear guard, gave them also a volley. Our cavalry then rushed out, charged and put the Frenchmen to flight, after wounding and making several of them prisoners. One of our horsemen led in a prisoner who had received a deep gash on the cheek: this fellow was so enraged with his conductor, that he poured forth torrents of abuse and oaths, such as '*sacre Dieu!*' &c. but the Englishman returned an answer for every imprecation, by giving him a thump across the back with the flat side of his sabre.

This 'brush' having removed us to a marshy part of the forest, we were obliged, for our own comfort, to cut down branches to sleep upon for the remainder of the night. An hour before day-light the army moved off, the 71st acting as a rear guard for the coming day: by dawn, our old friends, the French cavalry, could be seen indistinctly through a heavy mist, which still lay on the ground: two men were sent out to ascertain the reality of their approach. Before the scouts had proceeded a dozen yards, they were fired upon: this was enough. We immediately formed square and stood for some time, then moved on in the same attitude, leaving several drowsy stragglers behind. The French were still following with unwearied assiduity, although always kept well at bay by our gallant dragoons.

Still traversing this tiresome wood, we halted after crossing a river: a heavy firing was heard about this time, the enemy having assaulted the rear of Wellington's army, but without any material success. Our bivouac this evening would have been no way un-worthy of furnishing a subject for a painter: – figure to yourself, reader, a large body of men sitting on the ground amidst water, at least six inches deep, with rain descending upon them by bucketsful; fires, where any could be kept alive, sending forth volumes of smoke, and, at chance times, a transient gleam of flame, which only

---

[4] The 28th (North Gloucestershire) Foot.

served to illume for an instant our ragged raiment, stained haversacks, long beards, and way-worn countenances. Next morning we marched with alacrity from our 'lodgings on the cold ground', leaving several men unable to move, in consequence of cramp in the stomach. The road wound through the centre of lofty mountains, down the sides of which brooks, converted into torrents by the constant rain, fell with a brawling noise, making at the same time numerous streams across the road, every one of which we had to ford, often up to the middle.

We halted that night in security, our retreat being terminated; the enemy having given up the pursuit, chiefly, it is supposed, on account of our arrival in the vicinity of Ciudad Rodrigo. This was certainly a well-conducted and fortunate retreat: undoubtedly, no small loss and misery were experienced in it; yet how light in comparison were they to those of Corunna!

Parting from Wellington's army again, we marched to a village, which was universally denominated the 'smoky town' by the men, a continual smoke hanging over its crooked streets; yet scarcely so deleterious, I believe, as the pestilential vapours of the Glasgow and Manchester public works. Removing to the town of Coria, we received some arrears of pay; which were immediately squandered away upon wine; the kettles of that fascinating liquor never standing empty as long as the means of supplying them lasted. Our prodigality elicited a remark from a Spanish landlady which would have done no discredit to any 'thrifty auld Scotch wife', – she expressing her surprise that we spent so much money in wine, and never thought of buying shirts to our backs: in fact, it must be owned, that we were as ill, if not worse off, in this respect, than Falstaff's[5] famous

---

[5] A fat and boastful bon-viveur character created by William Shakespeare who appeared in both Henry IV plays and *The Merry Wives of Windsor*.

crew, – they possessed a shirt and a half, but we could not boast of one at that time!

From Coria we removed to Monte Moso, the most advanced post in the direction of the enemy's cantonments; here another draft joined us: it was in this manner that all-devouring Death required to be fed. New-year's-day, 1813, was spent with due honour, by carousing in the usual manner – the favourite song was the – 'Banks of the river Clyde': the allusion to home explains the cause of this, – for, of course, the uppermost wish of many was the desire soon to reach that haven, although such a prospect had not the remotest appearance of being realised, at least at that period. For my part, I almost wish, at the present moment, that Spain contained me still.

We next took up our quarters in Igal, a village situated near Placentia; our lodgings were more comfortable now, two of us only being billeted upon each inhabitant. One day, talking with the landlady of our house, she was asked, why she did not send her daughters to a nunnery? She replied, – 'Send them to be *putias*!!' viz. courtesans. It would be foolish and illiberal to take this solitary instance as the voice of the nation; but from other circumstances known to us, she was not far wrong in her opinions these seminaries of pretended religion.

About this time, the French had the boldness to send in a demand for a contribution from the people of Boho, a village at no great distance from us: the 50th were instantly despatched to occupy that place, – which was as much as to say – 'take it if you dare'. Quitting Igal, we shifted our lodgings to Puerto Banios, in the time of Lent; which, although it did not in any way interfere with our cooking operations, yet there is little doubt it would disturb those of the inhabitants. Lent seemed also to give rise to many processions and other Catholic ceremonies: I observed, in particular, a troop of boys, who were busily employed making insufferable noises with large clappers, to rejoice at the signal victory obtained by Michael over the devil, as I was told. Why should the superstitions of ancient Greece and Rome be laughed at? They yield not in absurdity to the story I have mentioned.

While we lay in Puerto Banios, a troop of wolves entered the village, and devoured a hog and a bullock; the neighbourhood was also so much infested by the wolves, that the alcalde gave rewards for bringing in their heads. It would appear that this had stimulated the Spaniards much, every door in the place being graced with the desired trophy. One morning, the rolling of musketry was heard in the direction of Boho. We immediately set off, full speed, to lend the 50th any assistance that might be required; but on our arrival at their quarters, it was discovered that the French had paid them a visit betimes, and had happily been beaten off. Soon after this the 50th and we changed places, we removing to Boho.

At that delightful place I got into exceedingly good quarters, being lodged in the house of a rich man, or at least a proprietor of several houses. I may say with safety, that from the day of leaving home I had never found real comfort until the hospitable Don Alphonso received me into his dwelling. His family only consisting of himself, wife, and daughter (a girl of thirteen), I, along with my comrade, dined with them every day – they cooking our rations. The excessive kindness of these benevolent people was the more acceptable to us after such a life of toil and misery. So solicitous were they for our welfare, that if we at any time happened to be later than usual in coming home, the landlord himself would search through the whole village, for the purpose of bringing us to the house.

Our stay in Boho rendered the place what is called 'extremely gay', the young women and our men getting very gracious: dancing formed an important part of the amusements. Even on Sundays the girls would come out into the streets, playing on panderas:[6] dances were then struck up, which many of the men joined in; others, more scrupulous, refrained on account of the day.

Summer approaching apace, active preparations began to be made for taking the field again: tents were served out, three to each company; kettles were also distributed, portable enough to be carried on the back. This was a wise regulation, we being enabled to commence cooking the moment a march ended; whereas, formerly, the kettles were of such an unwieldy construction, that they were obliged to be placed upon mules, which, by their tardy gait, were always far behind, and thereby kept us from our meals for many a grievous hour. Our regiment was reviewed here by General Stewart,[7] who, about the same time, performed an action for which we ever after held him in the highest respect. Seeing how much sentinels felt when bearing about a heavy knapsack, especially when exposed to the rays of a burning sun, he ordered that henceforth they should be at liberty to lay the knapsacks on the ground while on duty;

---

[6] A stringed instrument similar to a lute.

[7] Lieutenant General William Stewart was commander of the 2nd Division at this time. Wellington did not consider he was capable of independent command – nor of obeying an order. He was accused of badly mishandling the 2nd Division at the Battle of Albeura in May 1811. He was the first commanding officer of the Rifle Corps, later the 95th Rifles, and was known as one of the best battalion commanders in the British Army in the early 1800s. He was known to his men as 'Auld Grog Willie' for his habit of ordering extra issues of rum to the troops and their families. On at least one occasion he was forced by Wellington to meet the cost of the issue from his own pocket. Corporal Kermack in his reminiscence recounts how Stewart once gave his young daughter a dollar from his own pocket after coming across her as she watched her pregnant mother doing laundry for some officers. Kermack said the general told the girl, 'Here, cause your mother to get you something,' before remarking to an aide 'The poor women and children are miserable these times.'

saying, also, that there was always plenty of time to lift them, if any alarm should take place.

On the 21st of May we bid adieu to repose and the good people of Boho, multitudes of whom turned out to convoy us. Aged parents were seen running distractedly about, endeavouring to drag back their weeping daughters: every man of us had placed a handkerchief on his ramrod, as a kind of farewell signal. Notwithstanding the remonstrances of the old folks and Col. Cadogan himself, thirty young women obstinately persisted in attaching themselves to as many of our men. The colonel was unwilling to use force in getting rid of the women; but he hit upon an effectual method for doing so gradually, – this was by allowing them no rations. The paramours bore awhile with this regulation, through means of sharing; but times of scarcity coming on afterwards, a coolness took place on both sides, as might be expected; and the damsels dropt off by degrees, taking up with muleteers, or any one who could afford to feed them.

Having encamped for a few days in the vicinity of Boho, for the purpose of joining the other portions of the army that were assembling from the various cantonments, myself and a comrade took advantage of the interim to visit our bene-factor Alphonso. The worthy family received us with unaffected joy: we were invited to dinner; many a pressing invitation was given to me to return after *la guerre,* and make their house my home. I wish to God I had done so, – irrevocable circumstances prevent me now: besides, who knows if they are in the land of the living? But to return to the subject, – several Spanish soldiers had been quartered in the house since our departure; they, seeing us so well treated could scarce conceal their rage and envy; and all the time of the visit regarded us with very sinister looks: but the actions of such fellows were beneath contempt. The parting moment came at length: we took leave of Alphonso, the amiable Esperanza, and her mother, for ever, and returned with sorrowful hearts to the camp. Some may think it childish that I should mention that these almost strangers have been the leading characters in the drama of my dreams; and on these occasions they have seemed always to be near me, as I thought, while I never could obtain an opportunity of speaking to them.

But realities must be resumed; – it was not difficult to perceive that the efforts of the enemy had begun to slacken; and that their locust-like hosts descended seldomer into the Peninsula: the obvious cause of this arose, as it is well known, from the vast Russian expedition, which cramped every other operation.

We began our march northward, on account of the French abandoning the south of Spain without compulsion, – unless a decrease of numbers and supplies can be called so. The weather being exceedingly sultry at the first outset, one of the stoutest men in our company was so much affected by it as to fall suddenly to the ground in the throes of death, grasping at every object around him, and being quite insensible. He was placed in a waggon, where death ended his cares. We all ascribed this man's misfortune to a habit he had of wearing his cap too far off his forehead, and thought he must have undoubtedly been sun-struck. After passing Salamanca, we were joined by the Oxford Blues and the King's Life Guards,[8] from England: their finery, me-thought, should have saved them from the tarnishing effects of the Peninsular War. Tedious marches by day, and encamping at night, brought the whole army safe to the environs of Vitoria; the enemy had also concentrated their forces within three leagues of that place.

Some desultory warfare had taken place; but it was not till the 21st of June that Vitoria was numbered among our

---

[8] Six squadrons of the Household Cavalry were at the Battle of Vitoria. The 1st Life Guards, 2nd Life Guards and the Royal Horse Guards each supplied two squadrons.

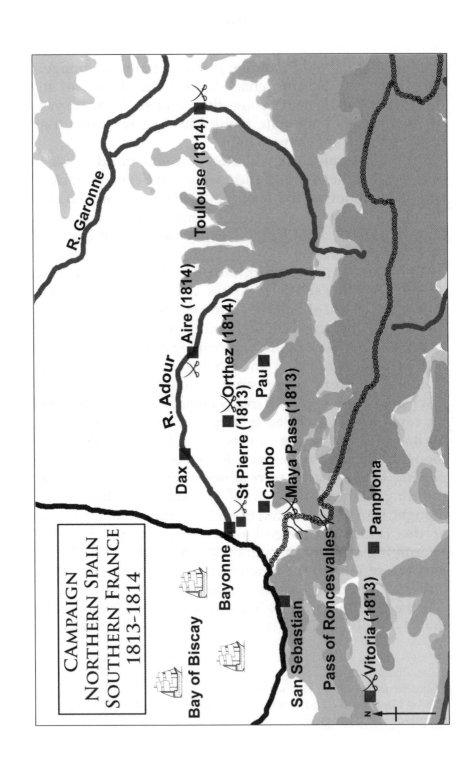

CAMPAIGN
NORTHERN SPAIN
SOUTHERN FRANCE
1813-1814

Bay of Biscay

R. Garonne

R. Adour

Toulouse (1814)

Aire (1814)

Orthez (1814)

Pau

Dax

St Pierre (1813)

Cambo

Maya Pass (1813)

Bayonne

San Sebastian

Pass of Roncesvalles

Pamplona

Vitoria (1813)

N

victories. On the morning of that day we halted, after passing through Puebla, and made preparations for battle: the cavalry and horse artillery being ranged along the front of the infantry, the march was then continued. While thus advancing, one of our Irishmen expressed his apprehension that the 71st would not have an opportunity of distinguishing themselves, and that there would be 'no mention of us in the newspapers'. Poor fellow, little did he know how soon we were destined to suffer more loss than any of the other regiments, and that his own death-wound was to be received in the fray.

Lord Wellington having contemplated the seizure of the heights of Puebla, where the left of the enemy's army was posted, the obvious executors of the project were the right of our army, which was as usual composed of Hill's division. It was not long before orders came to open out right and left, and for the 71st to advance. 'Come on, my lads,' said Cadogan;[9] 'come on, and get hairy knapsacks.'[10] We accordingly moved forward through the opening made for us, and soon had an unobstructed view of the whole French army, drawn up in lines: turning then to the right, we began the ascent of the heights. To have thus obtained the honour, as it were, of 'opening the ball', some may think ought to have made us what is called 'burn with enthusiasm': but I could perceive no such feeling, nor even common satisfaction: the only words uttered were invectives and murmurs at the steepness of the heights, and the slippery state of the grass. I knew that another regiment placed in our situation would have been an object of envy; but the fact is, fighting had begun to lose its novelty.

---

[9] Cadogan was commanding the 1st Brigade of the 2nd Division but decided to lead the advance of the 71st Highland Light Infantry rather than remain with the brigade's 50th West Kents and the 92nd Gordon Highlanders.

10. The standard-issue French knapsack at this time was made of goat or cattle skin with the hair retained on the outside.

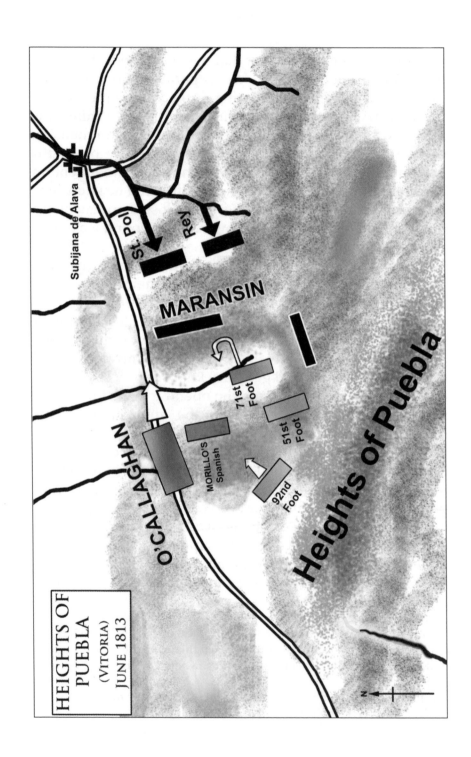

HEIGHTS OF
PUEBLA
(VITORIA)
JUNE 1813

Subijana de Alava

St. Pol

Rey

MARANSIN

O'CALLAGHAN

MORILLO'S
Spanish

71st
Foot

51st
Foot

92nd
Foot

Heights of Puebla

N

When the summit of the heights was reached, we found ourselves close to the enemy: a line was then instantly formed, and a volley fired, followed by three cheers. The enemy returned the fire, but soon began to retrograde; upon which we pressed on. It was at this important moment that the gallant Cadogan fell, as he rode along the front of the regiment. While in the very act of turning round to cheer us on, the fatal bullet had struck him between the haunch buttons: feeling the wound mortal, he desired himself to be carried to an eminence, where a full view of the engagement might be obtained: this request was of course complied with. Meanwhile, the command devolved upon Major Cother,[11] who still led us forward for some distance: liberty to halt was then given. One of the men succeeded in abstracting a loaf from the knapsack of a slain Frenchman: the generous finder coming to satisfy his own appetite, immediately distributed his treasure through the whole company: each had only a morsel, – but keen hunger rendered such a gift sweeter than honey.

A body of Spaniards, under the command of Murillo (the Tyrant of South America),[12] now marched by us to attack the enemy; soon afterwards we also moved on, three deep, along the ridge of a hill. Already it was evident that the Spaniards had found their enterprise too hot: many of them were to be seen skulking ignominiously to the rear, under various pretexts: some pretended a want of ammunition; others showed an affected solicitude for wounded men, by attending them carefully to a place of safety: four or five

---

[11] Major Charles Cother was acting commander of the 71st while Cadogan led the 1st Brigade.

[12] In 1814 Major General Pablo Morillo was sent to South America where he gained an unsavoury reputation for savagery while attempting to suppress the independence movements in several of the Spanish colonies. He had been captured by the British in 1805 while serving as an officer in the Spanish Royal Marine Corps at the Battle of Trafalgar.

men scrupled not thus to leave the field with a single wounded one, but the idea of returning never once entered their heads! A strong body of French, posted on a rising ground, began to impede our march by a destructive fire: almost every moment a man fell, either killed or wounded.[13] Disregarding the heavy loss, however, we succeeded in forming with our right under a rocky cliff, in a position rather higher than that of our opponents, which enabled us to return their fire with interest. It is somewhat remarkable, that for a long time during this sanguinary contest, a party of the enemy should have remained undiscovered, perched on the top of the cliff above us. These were the fellows that securely poured down a perpendicular fire, which had such fatal effects; the balls striking the men's backs, and going through their heads and ears. Such wounds would have appeared disgraceful in any other case but this. Major Cother received a wound; and I *myself* had the trouble of picking a bullet out of my trowsers, where it had lodged in the most complaisant manner, without even grazing the skin: another leaden-almond contrived to break the swivel of my musket!

The party, who may be said to have been preying on our vitals, were at length disclosed to view and answered with firing as well as our circumstances could allow, without doubt, they had hitherto found their safety in the noise, smoke, and confusion occasioned by the unabated raging of

---

[13] It was at this point in the battle that the 71st suffered their heaviest casualties of the day. Perhaps as many as 200 men were killed or wounded. The regiment's total losses at Vitoria were around 320 killed and wounded. Somewhere between 40 and 50 members of the regiment were captured by the French at Vitoria but were released in October when the fortress at Pamplona surrendered. Some reports say that the body of French which shattered the advance of the 71st had been mistaken for friendly Spanish troops. The French took advantage of the mistake to allow the regiment to approach to within close range before unleashing their first murderous volley.

our engagement with the main body. Meanwhile, the enemy in the plains, desirous of regaining the important heights which we had wrested from them, detached a column of 5,000 men, led, it is said, by both Joseph Buonaparte and Jourdan:[14] with this force they advanced to the assistance of their comrades, sounding their military music at the same time with great pomp. Our strong Italian no sooner heard the approach of the new assailants, than, saying hastily, 'I be damme if I stop here longer', he ran off to the rear with infinite speed: we were the less surprised at this, on account of us having always a much higher opinion of his strength than of his courage.

The enemy's reinforcement now came in sight, ascending the eminences beneath us. We immediately seized the opportunity such a situation afforded, by continuing to pepper them with murderous efficiency the whole way up. But the imprudence of standing the onset of such fearful odds being evident, we descended into a hollow, and scarcely was this well done, when the French formed on our old position. The 50th and 92nd, who had all the while remained in reserve, no sooner saw us clear of the enemy, than they opened a well-timed, but distant fire upon them. This was to favour our retreat across the hollow: the musketry ceased, however, the moment we joined the rest of the brigade. The enemy, awed by our imposing appearance, did not venture to advance a step further: thus was their intention completely thwarted, the conquered heights of Puebla being firmly retained in our possession.

It is time, however, to look at the cost of the achievement. On calling the roll about 400 of the regiment were found to be killed and wounded, among which was the exact half of

---

[14] Marshal Jean Baptiste Jourdan served as a private in the French army during the American War of Independence. He was referred to by his detractors as 'The Anvil' because he was beaten so often. He was Joseph Bonaparte's principal military advisor for much of the Peninsular War but his fellow Marshals often ignored him.

our company. Of the sixteen men who bore the kettles of the company, only three were present: it would appear, therefore, that the cooks had been particularly unfortunate.

The rest of the army, extending from our regiment to the extreme left, had, during the course of the day, obtained some splendid advantages; so much so, that about dusk a general and rapid retreat commenced along the whole of the enemy's line; upon which, every part of our army pursued with hasty strides. Our feelings were destined to experience a severe trial, in passing over the identical ground where our slaughtered comrades lay. As soon as the wounded were aware of our presence, they set up faint cries for water, to assuage the burning thirst which is the inevitable attendant of blood-gushing wounds; they even invoked our assistance by name. A young man, well known to me, implored my aid with the most piteous language: I had only time to ask in what place of the body he was wounded; the reply was, 'in the back', by which I knew that it was mortal. Another man, a sergeant, we saw in a sitting position, with both of his eyes turned out on the cheeks, a ball having entered the side of his forehead: he too was calling for water. Duty – inexorable duty – compelled us to shut our ears, to the horrible distress, and pass on as indifferently as if so many sheep bled in a slaughter-house.

Darkness caused a halt: the excessive fatigues of the day rendered this repose doubly acceptable. On examining my shoulder, I found it of an ebony colour, in consequence of the numerous rebounds of the musket.

The battle of Vitoria having terminated this evening, it is necessary to say something regarding it; but this something is only from hearsay, as might be expected. The aggregate number of the allied army was superior to that of the French: the loss on each side was about equal.[15] We made

---

[15] The French lost an estimated 8,000 men, the British 3,675, the Portuguese 921 and the Spanish 562.

few prisoners; but this was abundantly made up by the capture of their immense train of artillery, and all the rest of their military luggage; besides which, the victory enabled us to reach the frontiers of France, without suffering much molestation.

By the by, an officer and twelve men had been sent to bury the body of the lamented Cadogan, who had died on the hill, and had been carried from thence to the grave across a horse. The situation of that grave is only known to the interring parties, they having dug it hastily in the most convenient field that could be found. One would have thought that Cadogan's death should have created a greater sensation than it actually did; but when it is considered how uncertain and miserable our own lives were, our apathy will cease to be wondered at.[16]

Next morning, while we were busily engaged in baking and boiling a little flour, which we had received the preceding evening, the word was given to fall into the line of march. Our regiment either did not hear the command, or was not willing to hear it: this negligence caused our major's wrath to be kindled against us. He came up to the lines, and rode furiously along through the fires, overturning kettles, and committing a terrible devastation amongst the cooking apparatus. Having thus aroused us to a sense of duty, by the assistance of his horse's hoofs, we moved on gloomily enough, – not so much on account of the loss of our breakfast as of our friends; the late dreadful gap in the regiment having become more observable than before, on account of many marching side by side with strangers instead of well-known comrades; in fact, we scarcely knew our places in the ranks.

Passing by the town of Vitoria without halting, we began to observe that the road was strewed with innumerable written

---

[16] While admired as a brave man, Cadogan was not universally popular among his men, some of whom felt he was a glory hunter. Cpl. Kermack noted he kept a pack of hounds which 'he seemed more attentive to than the comforts of the soldier'.

A memorial to Colonel Henry Cadogan of the 71st was placed in Glasgow Cathedral after his death at the Battle of Vitoria in 1813. Monuments to him were also placed in St. Paul's Cathedral and Chelsea Parish Church in London.

papers and regimental books: these were certainly new features in the wreck of a flying army. Halting at night, amidst heavy rain, a new system of bivouacking was adopted: parties of three men sitting down on their knapsacks, close to each other, and a blanket being then wrapped round the trio, served to ward off the storm in some degree. The rain continued, without intermission, all the following day, accompanied by thunder and lightning. An officer and his horse fell victims to the fiery fluid[17]. We contrived, however, to reach the environs of Pampeluna, in spite of the muddy roads and raging elements.

The strong fortress of Pampeluna being still in the possession of the enemy, we encamped before it, in expectation of having some hot work at a siege. The garrison were to be distinctly seen, loitering about, and leaning over the walls, surveying us with great *sang froid*. But instead of the British, an army of Spaniards was intrusted with the siege. Leaving the camp, therefore we moved on towards the Pyrenees.

---

[17] Captain Masterman of the 34th Foot and his horse were killed by a bolt of lightning.

Chapter Eight

From the extreme length of the lofty barriers of France and Spain, – to wit, the Pyrenees, – it was judged proper for the allied army to divide into several parties, for the purpose of forming a chain of posts from a certain point to the edge of the Atlantic. One of these parties commenced the siege of St. Sebastian, a fortress situated at the western extremity of the chain; while we (Hill's army), on the right, advanced upon the valley of Bastan, to which three divisions of the French army had retired after the battle of Vitoria. These were, I believe, the only troops the enemy had remaining in the open field throughout the Peninsula. Having reached the valley on the 4th of July, the same words of command were given as formerly, 'Open out right and left, and let the 71st advance': at this we certainly sprung forward with great alacrity, and scrambled up a mountain's side to turn the enemy. The 50th and 92nd had advanced at the same time, but along the main road. They, contrary to every expectation, were engaged first, and even lost a good number of men; and had not darkness put an end to the affair altogether, we should have been assuredly participators in it. Next day, the army ascended another step of the great Pyrenean stair, the enemy retreating before us; we reached Alisore, where we enjoyed two days of repose. On the 7th, two brigades were

167

detached to drive the enemy further up the hills: the rest of the division kept advancing along the main road till dusk, when all of us halted, and bivouacked in a brushwood which fringed the brow of a mountain: strict orders to keep silent were given, and no fires were allowed to be lighted. So close were we to the enemy, that their talking could be distinctly heard. On rising, at daylight, a dense cloud or mist was still lazily resting around us, and even far below our situation: the altitude of our position explains this. A faint skirmishing soon commenced but still the French edged off, and eventually disappeared.

At length every difficulty was surmounted by our reaching and crowning the summit of the heights of Mayo; and every earthly care was banished for a while by the glorious view which burst on our eyes: the kingdom of France lay extended before us in all its fertile beauty. The arms were quickly piled and everyone abandoned himself to a variety of reflections. Five years of incessant toil had cleared the Peninsula of Frenchmen, and brought us to the borders of their country: but how meagre were these advantages when the vastness of the cost was considered! How much blood had been spilt, and how many taxes had been extracted, to gain that empty honour! The Portugueze soldiers were already gazing on the French territory with savage looks, and planning horrible revenge for the manifold cruelties which had been inflicted upon their country; but happily for the innocent people, proper steps were taken when we entered France to prevent their suffering for the crimes of brutal mercenaries.

In the midst of our reveries, the sight of some French troops exercising below, reminded us forcibly that we had labour yet in store. It was on the 8th of July that our tents were pitched along the heights; from that time to the 25th our employments were various: roads were constructed to drag the cannon easily about, and the trenches dug around the tents to conduct the dripping water away; this high atmosphere being extremely moist, from the continual passing and re-passing of clouds.

The 71st marched through the typical Pyrenean town of Elizondo on its way up to the Pass of Maya.

The floating suspicion of the French being less 'cowed' than was imagined by their late reverses, was fully realised on the 25th, when, by firing a signal gun, intimation of their approach was given.[1] Everyone flew to arms; and a company of ours was posted on a high peak, while the rest of us moved to the right, at which point the enemy, to the number of 30,000, was ascending from France. The 50th and 92nd had already begun the contest when we joined them. The hostile columns were now at no great distance: soon, therefore, we commenced a fire with all the vivacity which freshness inspires; cutting off such numbers of the enemy, that at one time we were almost led to believe they were retreating, from observing so many of their men hobbling to the rear wounded. But here we reckoned without our host; the enemy continuing to mount progressively, bearing their heavy losses with great bravery; and at length they gained the top of the heights, in spite of all our efforts.

Inferiority of numbers precluding all chance of our withstanding them with success, an immediate retreat took place; but at every rising ground the firing was renewed, – in short, the usual expression of 'disputing every inch of ground', might be applied with exact justice in this instance. The pursuit was so hot at first, that two regiments of the division were cut off from the main body, and would infallibly have been made prisoners, had not they, with admirable presence of mind, descended the mountain precipitately by an obscure road. Meanwhile the rest of us had a narrow escape. While passing the head of a road which went down to France, a strong body of the enemy was seen climbing up to join their comrades; a few minutes longer, and we should have been fairly enclosed between

---

[1] An inexperienced young officer in the 71st initially identified the advancing French as a herd of bullocks. But the 71st's Captain Archibald Armstrong, from Sligo in the west of Ireland, retorted, 'By Jesus my young fellah, you will shortly find these bullocks have bayonets on their horns!' The young officer was seriously wounded in the clash. For several months the soldiers took to jokingly referring to the French as 'bullocks'.

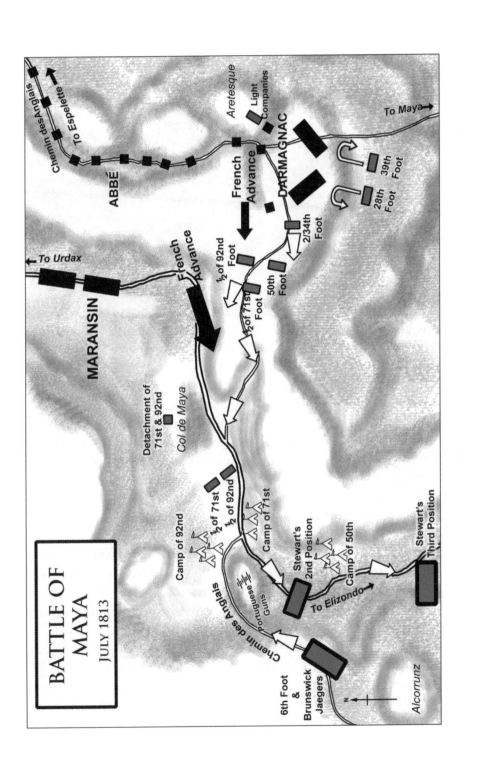

BATTLE OF MAYA

JULY 1813

To Urdax

MARANSIN

Chemin desAnglais

To Espelette

ABBÉ

Aretesque

Light Companies

To Maya

French Advance

DARMAGNAC

39th Foot

28th Foot

French Advance

½ of 92nd Foot

2/34th Foot

50th Foot

½ of 71st Foot

Detachment of 71st & 92nd

Col de Maya

½ of 71st

½ of 92nd

Camp of 92nd

Camp of 71st

Stewart's 2nd Position

Camp of 50th

Stewart's Third Position

Chemin des Anglais

Portuguese Guns

To Elizondo

6th Foot & Brunswick Jaegers

Alcorrunz

N

The path to the Pass of Maya from the French perspective. The road turns before it reaches the pointed peak and passes between the camps of the 71st and 92nd regiments.

the two. Reaching our camp ground, the 71st formed on the declivity of a hill for a short time; the rest of our little army, however, slacked not their pace, but abandoned the whole of the camp equipage, I believe, with the exception of our own company's, not a single tent was saved. General Stewart at length gave us orders to retire, which we did by marching round the foot of the peak where our company was posted; this small band was soon heard to be pouring down volleys upon the enemy's van, and successfully resisted every attempt to dislodge them by rolling down immense stones.

The enemy being again close at hand, a general stand was made, and the hottest engagement I have ever witnessed commenced; the enemy all the while endeavouring to surround us, their numerical superiority giving them every advantage for such a purpose; but this we evaded, by frequently shifting our position. We were now in a critical situation, the only hope of a safe retreat resting upon the approaching darkness: the appearance of a fresh body of troops, advancing from the west, also contributed to disconcert us – nobody knew what they were; but on General Stewart saying, 'Let us stand to the last', every one was confirmed in the resolution of still fighting on with energy. Happily for us, the dreaded foes turned out to be a reinforcement from Wellington's army, consisting of the 6th regiment[2] and the Brunswick[3] troops. It was rather a strange coincidence, that one of our men should at such a time recognise a brother in the ranks of the 6th, whom he had not seen for many years; the opportunity for mutual congratulations was short, scarcely extending farther than the mere shaking of hands. Nothing could have been more seasonable than the arrival of these regiments: they interposed between us and the enemy at a time when we were nearly overwhelmed, and began a heavy thundering fire. The French, however, were far from being backward in exchanging shots; as a proof of which, the major of the 6th fell lifeless from his horse at the very moment he had entered the field. The musketry only slackened in consequence of night-fall; and even then, the flashes served some for a marking point: at length, every noise but the groaning of the wounded was hushed, to the great relief of our deafened ears.

The woful duty of calling the roll next took place: the casualties were found to be numerous, particularly in our brigade, – for example, the 50th had 300 killed and wounded; the 71st, 200;[4] and the 92nd, 360: our loss, though it appeared inferior to the others, was, in fact, as much in

---

[2] The 6th (1st Warwickshire) Foot.

[3] The Brunswick units were mainly made up of non-French prisoners of war captured by the British. The nationalities represented in their ranks included Germans, Swiss, Dutch, Danes, Poles and Croats.

[4] The 71st reported fifty-eight dead and eighty-eight wounded as a result of the action on 25 July. A further fifty-three men are believed to have been captured by the French.

proportion; the Vitoria exploit having rendered us much weaker than they were. My company was reduced from 48 men to 11; I was, as usual, amongst the latter number, without having any thing to complain of personally; although a bullet-hole through my coat, and the cutting of the buckle-strap of my cartridge-box, spoke in silent but forcible language of the nearness of death, or wounds at least. At one period in the course of this eventful day, our ammunition ran so short, that three men in each company only could keep up a constant fire, they being supplied from their comrades' boxes: this plan was adopted to amuse the enemy for a while. It was about the same time that a Spanish muleteer was descried on his course up the hills, bringing a supply of ammunition; but no sooner had the man come near enough to the scene of action to witness its horrors, than he instantly wheeled round his mule and fled.

Some of the men had a hot chase after the poltroon before he was seized: by dint of mere dragging, they succeeded in placing him near the regiment: at that very juncture, the mule fell, wounded, to the ground. This circumstance, as might be supposed, did not contribute to raising the courage of the muleteer, who disentangled himself from the dying mule, and ran off with the swiftness of a roe, leaving us to disburden the cargo in what manner we chose. Habit is all-powerful: – inured to death and danger by long practice, the muscles of fear never once exerted their influence on our faces in the day of battle; but with an unconcerned spectator, such as the mule-driver, the case is different: war is not his trade, and self-preservation, the natural stimulus of mankind's actions, predominates in his mind. In the heat of the engagement, General Stewart having received a slight wound, and no surgeon being at hand, two of our men had the opportunity of rendering him a little service: they dressed the wound so much to the general's satisfaction, that he noted their names in a pocket-book, and afterwards presented one of them with three guineas; the other lived not to receive a reward.

Not choosing to bear the brunt of a second attack, we stole silently away in the dark: such of the wounded as could crawl followed us with difficulty, while those who could not, injured themselves more by useless, yet touching cries, entreating our protection.[5] This retrograding march to Spain, so contrary to expectation, threw a gloom over every mind: strong apprehensions were entertained that all our battles would be to fight 'o'er again;' not at our own firesides, but in good earnest. Had our pursuers been led by Buonaparte in all his pristine vigour, there is little doubt but that the suspicion would have been realised.

Soon after day-break, we met parties of cavalry going up, charged with the mission of carrying away the wounded to a place of safety: a good number of these unfortunate men were brought down across the horses' backs. Hardly had we encamped, when the appearance of the French caused the whole division to climb the sides of a mountain where some repose was obtained till the following morning, at which time the descent was continued till night, the old brushwood sheltering us once more. Here some of the men took advantage of the darkness to extract the rum-barrels from the commissary's mules; drinking and carousing, of course, followed; this led to the detection of the more incautious, who were slightly punished.

We still continued our march towards Pampeluna: a heavy firing was heard on the morning of the 30th; in fact, several

---

[5] Gavin in his diary makes mention of a company under a Lieutenant William M'Craw which the French believed they had surrounded and could be dealt with at leisure next morning. But M'Craw and his men managed to slip through the French lines and rejoin the 71st next morning. However, as M'Craw was reported to be a 'loose character', credit for the exploit was given to another officer and Wellington promoted him instead.

engagements had taken place of late, the enemy having penetrated into Spain at more than one point. In the afternoon, they appeared, advancing towards us in great force; upon which, two companies were posted in a wood, when a pealing of musketry commenced between them and the French. Our whole brigade was soon engaged; notwithstanding this, we were driven backwards to a range of hills, where quiet was at length obtained.[6] Upon this occasion, the Portugueze troops engaged the French, in a hollow, with the greatest bravery, and lost many men.

This continual mountain-warfare harassed us to an inconceivable degree; so much so, indeed, that death itself was eagerly panted for by many; others had serious thoughts of allowing themselves to fall into the enemy's hands. But the state of affairs began thenceforth to change: Soult's bold efforts to chase the allies from the frontiers of his country were now slackening for want of soldiers.

The next morning we resumed the offensive, attacking the enemy, who had retired under the covert of a brushwood jungle: some smart skirmishing ensued; but this Indian sort of warfare had its disadvantages, several of our men shooting each other as the intense thickness of the wood deceived their eyes. At length, the enemy were beat out of their shelter, and no more was seen of them until our invasion of France. General Stewart was severely wounded in this affair, yet in this state, while bearing through a camp, he, with his accustomed good-nature, ordered that every man in the division should have an extra allowance of rum.

Ascending the Pyrenees once more, we reached the heights of Mayo, the scene of our late conflict. After having

---

[6] The regiment lost a further twenty-four men killed and thirty-seven wounded in this action. Regimental records show that between 14 June and 7 August 1813 the 71st lost thirty-three sergeants, six buglers and 553 rank and file. On 7 August only twenty-one sergeants, fifteen buglers and 356 rank and file were recorded as being fit for duty.

reposed our weary limbs for some days, we moved through steep mountain-roads to the valley of Roncesvalles. A residence of three months here saturated us with stationary service, which must be understood was of a severe description. The principal events which took place in this were, the surrender of St. Sebastian and of Pampeluna to our arms; or, more properly speaking, to the arms of Sir Thomas Graham's[7] army, and those of the Spanish troops. Twelve men belonging to our regiment joined us from Pampeluna: they had been prisoners there ever since the battle of Vitoria. Starvation had reduced them to skin and bone, the French garrison having been subjected to the greatest straits for provisions before they submitted to the Spanish army.

Our own transactions in the valley of Roncesvalles were at least multifarious, if devoid of interest. We were engaged in the building of batteries and block-houses;[8] preparing shells to roll down mountains, without adopting the vulgar method of firing them from mortars: these occupations, along with hard duty, filled up our time for a while. The re-appearance of General Stewart, who had completely recovered from his wounds gladdened every heart: the

---

[7] Lieutenant General Sir Thomas Graham was a late-comer to military life. The 46-year-old Scottish nobleman raised his own regiment, the 90th Perthshire Volunteers, later the Perthshire Light Infantry, in 1794 and succeeded in persuading the young Rowland Hill to command it in the field. He served in Egypt in 1801, under Moore in Spain, at Walcheren, and commanded the British garrison at Cadiz 1810–11. His career was plagued and interrupted by frequent illness. He was appointed second-in-command to Wellington in 1812 but had to return to Scotland due to a problem with his eyes. He returned to Spain in 1813 and played an important role in Wellington's campaigns there. His military career ended on a low note when a force he commanded failed to take Antwerp in 1814.

[8] The blockhouses were made from wooden posts driven into the ground. Loopholes were cut and the blockhouse roofed. Each housed up to eight men, who were relieved after two weeks' garrison duty.

whole camp rang with the loud and hearty cheers of the soldiery. The uncommon noise alarmed many of the officers, who were for some time ignorant of its cause. Philosophical sneers may be elicited by this, and conclusions made, that it was easy to gain popularity among common soldiers by giving them a little rum and the liberty of walking for a short time without burdensome knapsacks. But these formed only a small part of Sir William's benevolent actions: besides, it was notorious to every one, that he never set baits for applause; – all proceeded from innate goodness of heart and not from weak and unworthy motives.

When the weather became sharp, each brigade of the army had week about of occupying the lofty heights of Altobispo. The climate of that peaked desert continued to wax colder and colder as the year advanced, its severity at length arrived to such a height that the artillery horses were obliged to be taken to the valley, being unable to endure the cold longer. About this time I was sent up: two of the days, in particular, were nearly insufferable: wind of the most tremendous violence blew with unwearied fierceness; no tents could be erected, for they would have been torn to ribands; even in attempting to speak, a serious inconvenience was felt, the wind filling the mouth; fires, when any of our men suc-ceeded in lighting them, were instantly scattered over the precipices. Judge, then, what our *comforts* must have been!

At length, General Stewart, with his customary attention and humane feeling, ordered that only pickets, instead of a whole brigade, were to remain on the heights. Nobody supposed that the French would have the hardihood to climb the sides of this 'howling wilderness' with a hostile intention; but here we laboured under a mistake; they did make an attempt. Fifteen men of our regiment happened to be on picket that day: instead of flinching from the unequal contest, they displayed such skill and resolution in attacking the enemy, that the latter thought proper to make a pre-cipitate retreat, the haziness of the atmosphere rendering them unconscious of their own vastly superior numbers: the fifteen men were rewarded with medals.[9] The morning of the day the snow came on, I was relieved, from picket in a strange condition; our greatcoats were frozen, as it were, into shining steel hauberks, lumps of ice hid our eyebrows and whiskers – the evidence of the eyes alone could convince us of the possession of our torpid limbs.

The picket which relieved us (57th men[10]) were still worse off: a heavy fall of snow commencing, the consequence was three of them died; and the rest had to be brought down on mules, inanimate and frost-bitten. The folly of keeping human beings on such a place being now evident, the guarding was discontinued: in fact, a picket of Esquimaux[11] would have been necessary for the service, if our authorities had persisted in retaining the post. The snow continued gradually to descend lower, even reaching our encampment in the valley: this circumstance soon constrained the whole division to remove to the village of Roncesvalles for shelter. The smallness of this place incommoded us not a little, the men being literally squeezed into every house, to the great annoyance of the poor inhabitants.

One day a party of us were summoned on fatigue, the ostensible purpose of our mission being to drag in the guns of a battery which lay at some distance, deserted on account of the snow. Some bullocks were provided, under the idea that they would tread a good road in the snow, and by that means facilitate the passage of the cannon.

---

[9] It had been believed that the French would not attack at this time due to bad weather and the natural strength of the British positions. Sergeant James Ross and his fourteen men not only fended off an attack by a force that vastly outnumbered them but forced it to retreat. Ross was still alive in 1847 to claim the General Service Medal.

[10] The 57th (West Middlesex) Foot.

[11] Also spelled Eskimo. The remaining indigenous population of Arctic Canada now prefer to be known as Inuit.

Furnishing ourselves all with sticks, we sallied forth, driving the cattle before us; but it was soon found that they were either too stupid or too headstrong to go abreast; in short, they dispersed several ways, in spite of our effort some of them even running nearly out of sight, in the deeper places of the yielding snow. To every appearance, the probability of having a bullock-hunt was much greater than that of making a road; when General Stewart detached me, along with five others to a distant block-house, in order to ascertain the condition of three men who had been posted there for some time. Leaving the dragging party, therefore, we set off, following the course of some lines which had been built in a French and Spanish war, twenty years before. When the end of them was attained, we used the precaution of breaking our sticks to pieces, and planting them in the snow, at regular intervals, on the whole way to the block-house, which was at length reached. The three men, however, were nowhere to be seen: it appeared afterwards, that they had evacuated the house, and returned by a different route.[12] Meanwhile, we were rather loath to return at once from the object of our errand: perhaps this commendable state of mind originated, in some degree, from the sight of a large quantity of biscuits and several little sturdy kegs of rum, with which the corner of the block-house was gracefully bedecked. After a long deliberation, in which the danger of drinking spirits in the intense cold, and the danger of being punished for pilfering them, were fully discussed. It was carried, by unanimous consent, that a little rum would be of service to us: this was enough; and ere long the liquor was gushing into a shoe, for want of a better dish. We had

---

[12] Gavin reported in his diary that during that winter the occupants of two blockhouses vanished completely and were believed to have been eaten by wolves.

the wisdom to quaff a small quantity only, at the same time feeding plentifully on the biscuits, to counteract any intoxicating effects: with the latter article we took care to stuff the lining of our coats, no haversacks being brought with us on this expedition.

Trudging off again through the snow, guided faithfully by the sticks, we had just arrived at the last one, when an officer of engineers appeared, accompanied by two of his men. He immediately desired us, in an authoritative manner, to go back with him to the block-house, and we, of course, were forced to comply with the command, although our reluctance was great, for more than one reason. Entering the house once more the officer, by way of a great favour to us all, ordered one of his men to saw a barrel asunder; part of the contents of the same rum keg we had been at was then poured into the empty half barrel: this unwieldy glass was raised to our heads with some difficulty. Having thus regaled us with rum, he extended his generosity so far as to bid us fill our foraging-caps with biscuits; we did so, chuckling inwardly at the same time at having anticipated him: but on his pointing significantly to a heap of shovels and pickaxes, and ordering us to carry them to the village, the cause of his courtesy was cleared up at once. Heaving up our burdens, we set off, groaning under their weight: one of the engineers having become inebriated, he fell with his load, and rolled over the snow, exposing at the same time his cargo of implements. This fellow's tongue consoled us, in some degree, for the officer's scurvy trick: he was so far from being awed by his commander, that he never failed to pour out volleys of abuse on him, at every interlude between the acts of rolling and rising up: this odd scene continued the whole way to the village, the officer stomaching all with astonishing meekness.

In the beginning of November, the plan for the invasion of France was put into execution. On the 8th of that month our brigade broke up from Roncevalles, and marched again to the heights of Mayo, the remainder of Hill's army had moved before us; we were therefore necessitated to advance hastily to the place of destination. There roads were horrible, and the way long, but no rest was given till the object was attained: snatching a hurried meal, we threw ourselves exhausted to the ground. The force collected here was numerous in my estimation, consisting of no less than 110,000 men, British, Portugueze and Spaniards.

Two hours after dark, the whole allied army began to descend into France: after marching for some time, a rivulet was crossed, – a glimpse was then caught of a French army, posted on the heights of Nivelle. They were instantly attacked, and the engagement became general: our brigade, however, was not troubled with firing a single shot, in consideration of their late harassing march, which the rest of the army had not endured, at least for some time previous. While this short action was going on, we remained in reserve, perfectly indifferent to the animated scene before our eyes; – so much had excessive fatigue benumbed our curiosity. A gleam of sunshine, the first we had seen for some time, now shone forth; and, stretching ourselves on the ground, the genial warmth was enjoyed as long as it lasted. The enemy having been discomfited, we took possession of their camp for the night. Certainly this camp was the most magnificent I had ever beheld: the exertions of both nature and art had been lavished in profusion. A party of French had taken advantage of our absence from Mayo to carry off some baggage, which had been left behind; but the activity of Mina,[13] the celebrated

---

[13] Spanish irregular leader Franciso Espoz Ilundian took on the *nom de guerre* Mina to associate himself with a distant relative of that name who had waged a guerrilla war against the French but had been captured in 1810. Ilundian was a peasant and a deserter from the Spanish army. His

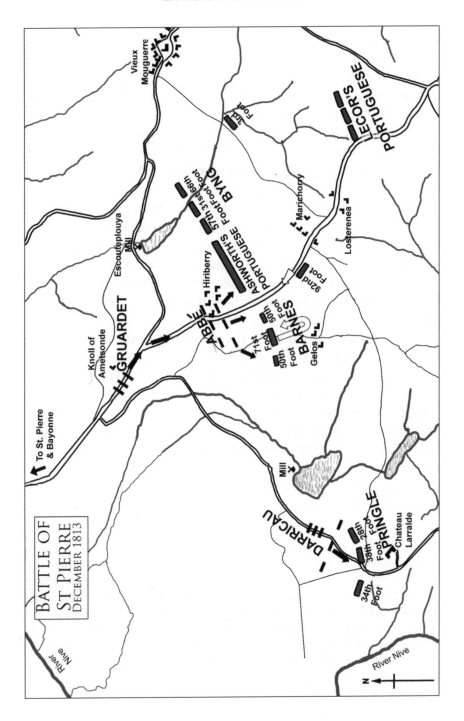

BATTLE OF
ST PIERRE
DECEMBER 1813

To St. Pierre
& Bayonne

Knoll of
Ametsonde

GRUARDET

Escouteplouya
Mill

ABBE

Hiriberry

ASHWORTH'S PORTUGUESE

57th 31st Foot Foot

66th

BYNG

3rd Foot

LECOR'S
PORTUGUESE

Mariehory

Losterenea

92nd Foot

BARNES

50th Foot

71st Foot

50th Foot

Gelos

Mill

DARRICAU

PRINGLE

28th Foot

38th Foot

Chateau
Larralde

34th Foot

River Nive

River Nive

N

Vieux
Mouguerre

Spanish chief, prevented any damage being done.

The army continued to advance unmolested on this powerful country, which had so long successfully resisted the approaching invader. After some days of exposure to heavy rains, our division reached the deserted town of Cambo, situated on the river Nive. Here we were quartered: the rest of the army were cantoned along the river, the French were also posted on its opposite side. Our regiment was strengthened at this place by the arrival of a draft.[14]

One day Wellington appeared in the town, and surveyed its situation and neighbourhood. We all knew this was the prelude to fighting, and prepared accordingly. On the same day the French sent down a regimental band to the edge of the river, and we listened attentively to every air they played. But next morning we rose before daylight, in expectation of another sort of music: our whole army was in busy commotion, preparing to pass the river. Leaving Cambo, our brigade marched up to a ford: the right wing of the 71st then lined the river and commenced firing, as did the other portions of the army at several crossing points. But, confining myself more minutely to our brigade's operations, – the left wing entered the river under cover of the heavy fire, and attained the opposite bank; the 50th and 92nd followed their example, and lastly, the right wing. Thus we found ourselves safe on *terra firma* again, without experiencing any greater loss than that of having a bugler wounded!

---

guerrilla band included Italian, German and Polish deserters from the French army. His force swelled in size until he was able to fight pitched battles against substantial French forces and lay siege to their fortifications in the Navarre region. Ilundian was given the rank of major general in the Spanish army. He was dubbed King of Navarre and clashed with the Spanish government when it attempted to reassert its authority in the region after the French pulled out of Spain. Ilundian was forced into exile.

[14] A draft of eighty-seven men from the 2nd Battalion of the 71st.

The resistance of the enemy was equally faint along the other parts of the river: in fact, they were distracted by the noise and extent of the different attacks. Next morning Hill's army moved on towards Bayonne: we quartered ourselves two days in its neighbourhood. Wellington's army had in the meantime retired across the Nive. The absence of such a large body of men encouraged Marshal Soult to issue from Bayonne, in hopes of crushing us before assistance could arrive. This movement brought on the battle of Bayonne, in which our division alone succeeded in defeating Soult, before Wellington's succours could come up. The success, however, was dearly, purchased, by a loss of 2,000 men killed and wounded, – among whom the 71st had a respectable number. For my part, I had not the honour of playing a part in the engagement, being all the while humbly employed in guarding General Barnes's baggage.[15] In the course of the

---

[15] The author's absence from the battalion may explain why, when he was so often critical of senior officers, he fails to mention the extraordinary behaviour of Lieutenant Colonel Nathaniel Peacock at the Battle of St. Pierre. Peacock had resumed command of the 1/71st after the death of Cadogan. At St. Pierre he ordered the battalion to retreat in the face of heavy fire from a brigade of French grenadiers. He turned his horse around and trotted to the rear. Major Maxwell Mackenzie countermanded the order but was killed moments later by a musket ball through the head. Some versions have 'Daddy' Hill personally leading the regiment back into the fighting. Peacock was later found harassing some Portuguese mule-drivers for fresh ammunition. Some accounts say Wellington himself confronted Peacock and ordered him to return to his regiment. Instead, Peacock rode over to join the 50th and 92nd who had pulled back out of range of the French. According to Gavin's diary, Peacock's trousers were holed by a French musketball and on the basis of this he insisted on being listed as wounded. Peacock was relieved of his command in April 1814 and cashiered. He was replaced by Lieutenant Colonel George Napier of the 52nd Foot, a great-great-grandson of Charles II and Louise de Kerouaille. Mackenzie's brother Colin was killed at Vitoria with the 71st. Their father John had been one of the 2nd battalion of the regiment's original officers when it was

day the general received a wound, as did each of his aides-de-camp, the Captains Hamilton: the brothers were brought to the rear, and orders given for us guards-men to bear them to a village at some distance. After placing the wounded gentlemen in blankets, we waded off through the midst of a knee-deep muddy road. Setting all boasting aside, I sincerely declare that the battle's hottest moment would have been infinitely more pleasant to me, and less degrading, than this errand: the opinion of the other bearers was, I believe, much the same. Arriving at the village, application was made for admittance at the first good-looking house that appeared. This request was haughtily refused by a diminutive-looking sergeant of the 36th, who stood in the portal with a seeming determination to oppose our passage, and saying, 'This is my colonel's house'. Too tired to spend more time in expostulation, we pushed the little man fairly aside, entered the house, and placed the captains in beds.[16]

On the ensuing day I was despatched with a letter to our brigade-major. Travelling alone, I fell inadvertently into a deep ditch by the way, – so deep, indeed, that I did not feel its bottom, on account of being fortunate enough to lay hold of a bramble bush in the descent. Grasping desperately at this support, I hung on, with my head only

---

formed in 1778. Their uncle Hugh was the 71st's paymaster and regimental tradition has Cadogan dying in his arms at Vitoria.

[16] Some of the 71st's wounded were housed on the ground floor of a barn and the upper floor was occupied by officers of the 92nd Gordon Highlanders. The officers heard one of the wounded shrieking and then being gently reprimanded in the following terms: 'Hold your tongue, James, and bear your fate like a man, for there are folk about us that may be hearing you. We'll soon both be at our ease; but in the meantime hold your tongue, and if you have no respect for yourself recollect what you owe the gallant 71st Highland Light Infantry, to which we both belong.' The shrieks ceased.

out of water, in no enviable state of mind or body either, as may be supposed. Happily, as I thought, some Spanish muleteers came in sight, approaching towards the ditch. I called loudly for their assistance: they raised their heads and gave me a vacant stare, continuing all the while to trot past very composedly without slackening the pace of a single mule. Whether it was indignation at such barbarous behaviour, or that Providence lent me aid, I will not decide; but at any rate I scrambled out, with no other damage than being completely drenched. Had not my firelock been in the same condition, I should at all events, have made a ball hiss about the ears of the cold-blooded miscreants.

Shortly after I joined the regiment, the army advanced towards the river Adour. We were then often billeted upon country houses. Once, when some officers were in one of them, and six of us in the adjoining stable (which, by the by, we had some trouble in converting into a sleeping chamber, on account of the floor being luxuriantly bestrewed with mire), a discovery was made of a kind which rejoices the generality of mankind. One of the men going about a pile of faggots in the yard, was attracted, by the peculiarity of its construction, to pull down some of the wood and step into the midst of the pile. Soon after, he cried for a bayonet, then a straw: these were handed in: the next accents were, 'I have found a whole barrel of brandy', When the discoverer had satisfied himself, we went in, and sucked through the straw by turns; taking the utmost care, at the same time, to escape the officers' observation, for obvious reasons. As fate would have it, however, a soldier from another house suddenly entered the yard, for the purpose of visiting us. We received him as placidly as possible; but he must have either remarked our anxious glances at the faggots, or heard the fidgeting of the man who was amusing himself with the straw: perhaps both causes urged the prying stranger to run to the aperture and find out the mystery: thus he compelled us, as it were, to "go snacks' with him. After we had retired to roost in the stable, this ungrateful fellow divulged the secret to his comrades, and guided them to the spot: what they did there may be guessed; but in addition, they had slipped off and left the spigot of the barrel on the ground, by which means the liquor rushed furiously from the hole, and nearly overflowed the yard. The gurgling sound awakened me in the middle of the night: we got up and stopped the running, but it was almost too late. Next morning, when we came back from parade, the powerful effluvia of the spilt brandy was sensibly felt: this alarmed us not a little. The certainty of being called to account for the transgression, prevailed in every bosom; and the idea of the officers' olfactory nerves winding the smell, was never once doubted. But, by a lucky thought, our terror and the smell were quashed together, by merely turning wet straw and mire over the dreaded places. The process was disgusting enough, to be sure; but the complete success of the scheme smoothed all the wrinkles of aversion.

We now marched to the banks of the Adour, and from thence to the town of Ort, on the same river, where our quarters were established till the month of February. The causes of this delay were derived from various circum-stances, such as heavy rain, and the consequent dreadful state of the roads. Indeed, the condition of the muleteers was a convincing proof of this, these men coming into the town regularly so be-spattered with mud, that they had actually more the appearance of being composed of clay than of the ordinary human materials – which, by the by, are also called clay. But the kind I allude to was of a different description, – it only covered the surface of the muleteers' persons: this crust, however, might have been several inches in depth. We ourselves did not escape the miry contagion, on account of the very severe duty which all of us were liable to on this post. There was seldom even time to doff our garments, to say nothing of washing them in the usual manner. We generally pursued the antediluvian system of washing, that is to say, walking into a river, and scrubbing only externally, – yet, strange as it may seem, colds or coughs were almost unknown to us: the constant exposure to fresh air will perhaps account for this.

Some French gun-boats used to take advantage of dark nights, to pass the town in their course to and from Bayonne: in day-light, or even moon-light, they never appeared. Although the French sailors took the precaution of using muffled oars, our pickets were too vigilant not to harass them by a random fire: this sometimes drew a return shot from the gun-boats. The house where our captain lodged was once struck by a weighty ball, – it passed through a clock-case, and drove in the wall of the room where the captain lay in bed, nearly burying him in a shower of mortar and rubbish.

One day the enemy landed on a small island on the Adour, where three of our companies were posted. After a smart contest, our men were driven by superior numbers from a large château, which in fact, was the only defensible place on the island. That night 100 of us crossed to their support. From the quietness of the enemy, thoughts already began to be entertained that they had quitted the island; but to set the matter at rest a patrole was detached to reconnoitre the château. They soon returned to say it was deserted. Relying upon the idea of our former suspicions being right, a picket of twenty men was sent to occupy the château; whence five of us were sub-detached, to quarter ourselves in a farm-house, which had formerly been used as a sort of out-post. By mere chance, a man of our small party happened to be on terms of intimacy with a girl of the house which we were going to. When we arrived at the place of destination, he therefore led the way, and tapped at the window, – the same, I presume, that he had before lurked about, on a different errand from the present one. After some interrogation, the casement was softly opened; the girl and her mother then appeared: a serious conversation

189

immediately commenced between them and the gallant, who spoke the French language very fluently, from his having been once a prisoner. We scarcely understood a single word; but it was easy to perceive that symptoms of strong alarm were depicted on the countenances of the females. At length it was interpreted to us, that a strong party of French soldiers were quartered in a house only a few yards distant! This intelligence surprised us a little; but being unwilling to retrace our steps in such a dark tempestuous night, we stood irresolutely pondering whether to remain or fly. The young woman now offered to go to the dreaded house, on some pretext or other, and ascertain the number of the foes. She went accordingly, and soon returned, after having discovered that they consisted of an officer and sixty men. Reckless of the danger, however, we entered the house, and expressed our determination to keep snug till the morning, not withstanding the good creatures' entreaties to save ourselves. Indeed, such unaffected anxiety for our preservation astonished us not a little; and what could be a nobler instance of courageous hospitality than the peasant girl's not delivering us into the hands of her countrymen? She realised, in fact, the masculine though fictitious heroines of the Waverley novels.[17]

We had taken the precaution of placing a sentinel under a tree: when this duty came to my turn, I could perceive a French sentinel close by me, walking to and fro in the usual manner. He stopped once – I grasped my musket firmer; – but it was to light his pipe with a flint and steel: a great noise and jabbering could also be heard, which arose from the Frenchmen in the house. Before day-light came in, we prudently resolved to steal off: but in the execution of this, our good fortune only partially continued; the enemy observing us and giving chase, firing at the same time several shots. But trusting to our heels, we soon gained the

---

[17] Written by Sir Walter Scott.

château, where the fifteen men were already stationed at the windows, ready to repel any assault, they having been roused by the musketry of the pursuers: but they, on the other hand, seemed to have stopped in their career, and evacuated the island, as we saw them no more.

I have mentioned the boisterous weather we had endured ever since the invasion of France. People who have been accustomed to read of the 'laughing climate' of the south of France, will scarcely recognise my poor description to be of the identical part which is so heavenly in their imaginations. To be sure, it must be allowed that the winter of 1814 was severe through the whole of Europe; but the glowing accounts of southern French, Spanish, and Italian winters are in general false. Their summers are indeed different from ours; yet, after all, the climate of the whole earth is, in my humble opinion, more alike than most travellers care to own.

191

Chapter Nine

The month of February saw the army again in readiness to push its conquests further into France. Our brigade left Ort, and after having had a slight skirmish with the enemy, we marched on till the evening and encamped. A French store lying exposed in the neighbourhood, some of the men entered it, and possessed themselves of a quantity of bread. I was first warned of this by seeing the depredators hurrying along, each bearing an immense loaf: the 92nd men had theirs wrapped up in the tails of their kilts! In the impulse of the moment I ran down to the store, but at a most unlucky time, the brigade-major having just arrived. On perceiving him, I stopped short, and immediately retreated, with as unconcerned an air as possible; this would not do, however; the major was too sharp not to discern the purport of my errand, – so raising his voice, he called for me to halt. But lending a deaf ear to the command, I only increased my pace, – upon which the vindictive major put spurs to his horse, with the hope of seizing me. My being overtaken was now certain, had I not had the presence of mind to ascend a rugged hilly path, impervious to the horse: this stratagem saved me. It was then I had time to blame myself for running headlong into such a scrape; and, perhaps, the idea of still wanting a loaf did not tend to decrease my chagrin.

On the following morning our army moved off; two companies of us, the German riflemen, and the light companies of the other regiments, being in advance. It was drawing near night when the enemy were discovered posted along the brow of a mountain, upon which we, the light troops, sat down on the face of a rising ground, – the rest of the army halting at the same time. The hostilities of the day commenced by the British artillery making several discharges upon the enemy. From the contiguity of the surrounding hills, the reports of the cannon were of the loudness of thunder. Perhaps it was this circumstance that induced an Irish officer of ours to express himself thus: 'Blood an' ouns, Mister M_d, are these our kenun!' On Mr. M_d assuring the brave lieutenant that they were, he seemed much comforted. This *jontleman* was at all times the standing joke of the regiment, chiefly from his uncouth form and tremendous brogue, – another example of which may be given. Seeing a sergeant with a telescope in his hand, he accosted him in this manner: 'Och, *sarjant*, will you lend me the loan of your spy-horn glass!'

But to return from the vagaries of the poor Patlander.[1] The light companies were now ordered to advance upon the enemy: we did so, and met their light troops, or tirailleurs, half-way between the respective armies. A severe skirmishing then took place. This system of fighting is of course already well known; but I may say, that although the combatants are in a scattered state, and take aim at each other, yet they very seldom know when they drop their men, – to speak in sportsmen's slang. The reason is obvious; – so many firing at the same time, and that often obliquely. In this, as well as in other skirmishes, we had occasion to admire the steady coolness of the German riflemen: these fellows never took the pipe out of their mouths, but fired away, as if they were only engaged at some ordinary

---

[1] A derogatory term for an Irishman.

194

occupation. The tirailleurs continued to retire gradually before us, and eventually fled for protection to their main body. Our enthusiasm not permitting us to wait for support, we rushed up the hill regardless of the heavy fire which the enemy poured down from the top of it. When the part of the mountain was attained, they descended on the opposite side. By this time it was quite dark; we halted accordingly, the rest of the division then came up and encamped. Our loss was less than might have been expected from such a smart brush.

Next morning 100 of us were detached to a village, for the purpose of observing the enemy, who were posted on the opposite side of a river. We stood for a considerable time in the village street, which gave the French inhabitants an opportunity of displaying their usual benevolence. They actually came out, took the canteens off our backs, and replaced them full of wine. When our commanding officer endeavoured to prevent such attentions, the worthy people watched till his back was turned, and then resumed. How different was this from the conduct of some French soldiers! disregarding the ordinary punctilios of war, they fired across the river, and shot one of the 13th Dragoons dead in our sight. This unfortunate man was on guard. Our indignation at this action was no way decreased on seeing another dragoon, a young Englishman, burst into tears at the fall of his comrade. He hung over the lifeless body for a long while, absorbed in grief, telling us also that the deceased had been as a father to him, and that the poor man had been upwards of twenty years in the regiment, respected by all who knew him.

General Stewart now came up and took forty of us across the river. While fording, we observed the water to be full of flour in bags: the enemy had probably thrown them in there, to prevent their falling into the hands of the British. Nothing of importance resulted from this reconnoitering. On our coming to a place where two roads struck off, I was stationed, along with another five men, to guard one of them: the rest of the party advanced along another road so far as to skirmish with the enemy, and to suffer a loss of two men, who were made prisoners. The division soon afterwards forded the river and joined us. Marching on again towards Salvaterre, we came in sight of another river, with the enemy drawn up along its banks. Our artillery immediately opened a dreadful fire upon their ranks, under cover of which the 92nd and two of our companies entered the river. It was about this time that General Hill's horse was killed by a cannon-ball. The general falling along with the animal, in sight of almost the whole division, a momentary gleam of concern passed over every countenance: but this was soon dispelled by his rising up unhurt. The death of General Hill would have undoubtedly been deplored by us all, so universally was he esteemed: in short, the highest eulogy that can be paid him is, to say that he was no way inferior to General Stewart in the greatness of soul and goodness of heart.

The 92nd having arrived on the opposite shore, and the rest of the division being busily employed passing the river on the beams of a wooden bridge, the planks of which had been taken away, the enemy took to their heels: we then occupied a village for that and the following day. Continuing our march, not a day passed over without skirmishes taking place. Fording also formed a necessary but troublesome part of our labour, this district of France being intersected with innumerable streams. At one time, while preparing to cross a very rapid one, a tall fellow must needs display his wit at the expense of another, whose stature could not be much vaunted of, saying, that he would carry him over dry by fastening him to his brush and pricker. But, after all, it was amusing enough to find that the wit was the only one in the whole regiment that required assistance, he having stumbled, and been saved from drowning only through the exertions of his comrades.

Arriving in the vicinity of Orthes, we encamped within a mile of the river Gave. Soult had now concentrated his army in front of Orthes, with the hope of stopping our farther progress. One day we made a feint by marching along the stream; but it was not till the following day that the intention of crossing was put into execution. Wellington's army was entrusted with the attack of the enemy's right and centre, while we were ordered to do as much for their left, which was commanded by General Clausel.[2] Marching, accordingly, towards the Gave, we crossed it under cover of both artillery and musketry, with so much success as to have only one of the 71st wounded; the other regiments of the division suffering equally little. Continuing our march, we arrived at the summit of a rising ground, and there halted.

Close by us stood a house and a small wood: out of these sheltered places a party of French kept up a galling fire; – the men were falling every moment: this threw every one into a sort of fidgetty state of anxiety to close with the enemy; – in fact, unseen destroyers generally produce such an effect. Two companies of our regiment at length received permission to chastise the lurkers; and instantly rushing down, they drove them out of the wood in a few seconds. The remainder of the enemy in the house were as yet unaware how things stood with their comrades of the wood. This gave an opportunity for a young lad, named Jack, to take his station at the side of the house-door The eyes of the whole brigade were now fixed upon the movements of the robust youth, when one of our band-men[3] suddenly breaking loose from those who endeavoured to restrain him, ran down to the house wielding a stretching-pole, and

---

[2] General Bertrand Clausel was commander of the Army of the North (sometimes referred to as the Army of the Left) at this time. He had previously commanded the Army of Portugal, in 1812.

[3] The bandsmen of the 71st were employed as stretcher bearers. The man referred to is believed to have been a bassoon player.

placed himself on the other side of the door. The un-suspecting Frenchmen at length began to issue from the door, unconscious of the fate that awaited them. Immediately, Jack, with his firelock and M'Rae with his pole, laid every one that appeared sprawling on the ground; if any were so fortunate as to escape the gun, they infallibly felt the weight of the pole; and *vice versâ*. A number of prisoners were thus secured, by the mere exertions of these two. Jack was made a corporal upon the spot; but poor M'Rae went unrewarded, he having little more than his valour to recommend him.

Moving on again, we came to a small village, where some partial skirmishing enlivened the scene. Our brigade then formed into close column. Soon after this evolution, a body of troops came in sight, advancing along a road: their steps were hasty and agitated; but they were suffered to pass us unmolested, we having no doubt of their being Spaniards. It was not long, however, before the mistake was rather unsatisfactorily explained, by the appearance of a Scottish brigade[4] (the 42nd,[5] 79th, and 91st) coming down the same road, playing furiously on their pipes, in full cry of the French, our supposed Spaniards. This discovery galled us to the quick; the fugitives having been completely at our mercy. But if they escaped from the infantry, they did not from the British cavalry; for, on looking round, we could see the country covered, as far as the eye could reach, with the broken and flying enemy: our horsemen were following them close, committing dreadful havoc upon such as did not halt and throw down their arms. The field of Orthes having thus been decided, we encamped for the night, and next morning pursued our march, passing, as usual, quantities of military wrecks. I remarked, in particular, a place where

---

[4] Commanded by Denis Pack, who led the 71st in Argentina, and at Fuentes de Onoro, Corunna and Walcheren; now a major general.
[5] The 42nd (Royal Highland) Foot, better known as the Black Watch.

several roads united: here immense heaps, or rather hills, of knapsacks, belts, caps, and canteens, lay piled on each other: they had, probably, been thrown down by the enemy that they might accelerate their flight.

At one time, a number of us happening to be quartered on a farm-house, its inmates supplied the most rapacious of our band; gratuitously, with a quantity of bread. A hen-roost, which stood in the yard, excited much attention: its inhabitants were, I believe, roughly treated; nay, even a sergeant was detected by the farmer in the very act of twisting a fowl's neck. Stripes was a little nonplused at the rencontre; but having the presence of mind to say that he had found a dead hen, the honest farmer only good-humouredly replied, that 'it must have died *per force!*'

The night before the battle of Aire took place, while a number of us were carousing over abundance of wine and brandy, R_h, an intimate friend of mine, remained alone, gloomy and silent: we were the more surprised at this, as he had been always hitherto, the blithest of a jolly company. On the following day, while we were advancing to engage the French, I walked alongside of him, but still he was morose and unaccountably silent; in fact, his former free and generous temper seemed to be entirely gone. We now parted – alas! forever. The troops having halted for a short time, General Stewart desired a sergeant to place a sentinel at the gate of a large château which stood hard by; and this job falling to my lot, the general ordered me to admit none but General Hill's staff. Meanwhile, the generals Hill and Stewart entered into deep conversation; aides-de-camp were continually passing out and in, bringing and carrying intelligence. One of them I particularly remarked, – Colonel Hood, of the guards; he was often examining a chart of the country, in addition to his other duties: this gentleman was soon afterwards slain in the engagement.

During this animated scene, an elderly Frenchman, an inmate of the château, scraped an acquaintance with me by asking for a small bit of tobacco. Having immediately gratified his request, the 'faithful old domestic' disappeared, and soon returned, bearing a large loaf and a jug of wine. The loaf being too unwieldy to go into my haversack in a lump, he took the trouble to break it down piece-meal, and cram it into the bag. As this action would have seemed improper in the eyes of the two generals, the old man carefully hid his treat when their faces were in our direction, and pretended to look at the army; but the instant their backs were turned, he continued his kind exertions.

The division having at length moved off, and my business being ended, I ran hastily on to join the regiment, taking short cuts through some fields to effect this the sooner. The noise of musketry beginning to burst on my ear, I did not relax in speed till a river stopped the way; but seeing a horseman fording it, I followed him, and reached the opposite shore in safety, after having been once nearly swept away. Joining the regiment in the midst of a severe skirmish, I was surprised to see one of our men with a long red feather stuck in his cap: on asking him the cause, I was informed that the unfortunate R_h had fallen a victim to the first shot in the engagement, and that he (the informant) had succeeded in shooting the French grenadier who had done the deed: the seizure of this man's feather was, therefore, intended as a sort of proof of revenge; – another instance of deadly forboding was thus exemplified. The skirmishing continued still to rage with unabated fury: it is to be understood, however, that our force consisted only of two 71st companies and the light companies of the other regiments; the rest of the division having gone to attack the main body of the enemy, who were posted upon a range of hills. I was, as usual, fortunate this day, having only received a ball through my trowsers; another tore up the ground underneath my shoe: the latter accident made some around me conjecture that I had at length caught a wound, – they were deceived, however, and I had still the appellation of 'lucky'. Indeed, a *fétiche*[6] would always have been a super-fluous article with me.

Our opponents having been worsted, towards night-fall it was agreed that we should quarter ourselves in the town of Aire, the rest of the division being encamped at some distance, on the field of battle. This part of the army had succeeded in routing the enemy, after an arduous conflict, in which M'Rae, our heroic musician, fell to rise no more. This strange being was far from possessing the ordinary coolness of Scotchmen. Although his profession absolved him from intermixing with the combatants, – yet on hearing the noise of an engagement, he seemed to be seized with an irresistible fury, catching up a pole or a firelock, and rushing into the thickest of the fight, dealing blows with the greatest force and efficiency. But fate cut short his career at Aire: he had there even exceeded his former valorous exploits, having levelled many a foe with the aid of his trusty pole; but just as he was poising it on high, to ensure a weighty blow upon a French soldier's skull, the man anticipated him, by firing the shot which stretched him lifeless in the dust. Certainly it may be said of the doughty M'Rae, that 'swords he smiled at, weapons laughed to scorn'.

On entering Aire, the first conspicuous objects that struck our eyes were two carts full to the brim of hams: little ceremony was used in helping ourselves to them all! No billets were served out here, every one entering the house that suited him best; but the inhabitants bore the oppression with great good-nature. In the house where I was lodged, along with some others, the people pointed out to us some clean beds to repose upon; but as we had been ordered not to take off our accoutrements, the offer was refused: whether or not, our tremendously muddy state would have prevented us from trespassing so far on their politeness as

---

[6] A good-luck charm.

to befoul the beds. We made ourselves very comfortable on the floor, with the help of a little straw.

Next day we marched out of the town to join our respective regiments, and had the trouble of coming back along with them. The streets of Aire were strewed with the bodies of French soldiers, who had been wounded in the divers engagements and had only strength to drag themselves into the town – there to die.

At one time, an officer of ours, a Mr Cox,[7] said to me, that I might take as many men as I chose to go out and bury R_h; but a pioneer, overhearing the discourse, assured us that he had buried the poor fellow: this serves to shew how much the deceased was esteemed by men of all ranks in the regiment.

Having been joined by a draft of 200, we left Aire, and journeyed towards Pau: after halting a day or two in its neighbourhood, a movement was made in the direction of Toulouse. We made an attempt to lay a pontoon bridge over the Garonne, but without success: we were obliged to construct it farther up the river. A long march was next provided for us, and we returned to the place of starting, after marching at least fifty miles without resting, – but perhaps this walk was necessary to alarm the enemy. We next marched to a place within two miles of Toulouse, where the inhabitants had fled: their wine-cellars remained, however, of which many of us could have given a minute description.

On the morning of the 10th of April we advanced towards the city, or rather the St Cyprien suburbs, which are situated on the west bank of the Garonne. The enemy had a battery of ship-guns here, which were sometimes discharged at us, but with poor effect: in fact, it may be said of our division,

---

[7] Lieutenant Charles Cox had been shot through the lungs at Vitoria and captured by the French. But he was abandoned during the French retreat and later served at the Battle of Waterloo.

that only a few light companies were engaged. Wellington's army having crossed to the Toulouse side of the river, by far the hottest part of the engagement raged there from morning till night, we had little more to do than listen to tremendous firing. It is said that the Spaniards behaved with astonishing bravery: they had certainly much need to do so, if it were for no other reason than to wipe off their former reproach. To make a long story short, the battle of Toulouse terminated in favour of the British, thus Soult's last expiring blow completely failed.

Next morning the division marched through the city: immense crowds of well-dressed people stood at a bridge to welcome us, or at least pretended to do so: all of them wore white cockades.[8] Another group was busily employed in pulling down a statue of Napoleon from the top of a triumphal arch. As we advanced farther into the place, almost every window was filled by ladies waving handkerchiefs. Fortunately for the 50th and 92nd, they had lately got new clothes, – their appearance; therefore, was passable in the eyes of the French; but as for us and most of the other regiments, any thing like magnificent costume was out of the question. Our clothes were in fact worn out; but not a rag hung, pennant-like, in the air, strict orders having been issued to that effect, although full liberty had been given to mend the holes with any sort of cloth. This indulgence was acted up to in the fullest extent – patches of canvass and of blankets covering us from head to foot, interspersed throughout with other patches, of all the colours of the rainbow: such habiliments had a very harlequin, mendicant effect. With regard to our personal appearance, many were tanned and weather-beaten by the long exposure to sun, frost, and rain; but the late drafts, of

---

[8] The white cockade was a symbol of the Royalists clamouring for the return of Louis XVIII.

course, were much less so. I may remark here, that the Portugueze were now much finer-looking soldiers than the generality of the British: the cause of this arose from the immense number of striplings which filled the ranks of the latter, while the Portugueze were almost wholly composed of full-grown, sturdy fellows.

On emerging from Toulouse, we directed our steps to the side of the Languedoc canal and there encamped. While on parade at another place, intelligence arrived of the northern allies' entry into Paris, and the subsequent deposition of Napoleon. This news diffused universal joy: a busy hum of delight ran round every rank; home and friends only were talked of, – for who cared a fig for the affairs of France? But still in expectation of fighting, we moved on to Ville Franche; old Soult being as yet resolved to consider us enemies to his country. Such conduct in a Blucher[9] has been denominated 'heroic patriotism'; but in our opponent it received the name of 'stubbornness', or 'a thirst of blood'.

A flag of truce at length arriving for the suspension of all hostilities, we marched back to Toulouse. Our stay in this city extended to about six weeks: the whole of this time was spent in the most agreeable manner, the inhabitants being friendly, – the provisions and liquor 'dog-cheap'. One night an illumination was ordered; but it turned out to be of a very paltry description, – a single candle in each window forming the average number of lights.

Preparations being made for the public entry of the Duc d'Angoulême,[10] our brigade, with some Portugueze,

---

[9] The notoriously tenacious Prussian Marshal Gebhard von Blücher.

[10] Louis Antoine, the nephew of Louis XVIII of France and cousin of Ferdinand VII of Spain. He served alongside Wellington in the closing months of the Peninsular War. His father succeeded Louis XVIII and ruled as Charles X. When Charles abdicated in 1830, Louis Antoine ruled France for 20 minutes, as Louis XIX, before also signing an instrument of abdication. Father and son went into exile in Edinburgh.

were called out to assist the National Guards in lining the streets. It must be understood, however, that we exchanged our former scare-crow dresses for good substantial clothing, previous to this 'august ceremony'. People of rank are well aware how much their importance is increased by the easy method of keeping the rabble, for days or hours, in momentary expectation of their arrival: the truth of this we and a large crowd besides found, having stood from morning till the approach of dusk, waiting for the duke's arrival. The duke, at last appeared, surrounded by an immense suite of officers, both French and British: they passed under a triumphal arch erected for the occasion. A faint cheering was heard at times among the citizens, but the National Guards were extremely vociferous, – however, the subject is too stale to admit of comment. We had another job in lining the streets, on account of a grand ball being given to the British officers and French nobility. When the duke was leaving Toulouse, we turned out and saluted him: that day chanced to be the anniversary of the battle of Fuentes de Honoro; every one of us had, therefore, a sprig of laurel stuck in his cap. I have little doubt but that the poor duke considered these decorations intended solely to do him honour.

Twelve of us were once hired to perform dumb parts in a theatre; this was assuredly my first and last debut. When the place was reached, we were all gorgeously dressed, the play being some grand eastern spectacle or other. Our first labour was to bear a princess across the stage in a palanquin, or at least in one of those gilded hand-barrows which pass for such in playhouses: some of us also wielded formidable-looking tin pikes as the princess's guards. But the most comical part of our operations was, to be furnished with wooden instruments, and perched on a balcony, to have the resemblance of a second orchestra. We did every thing in our power to aid the views of the manager, by seeming to blow with great musical taste upon his instruments. One fellow in particular, aped the actions of a musician in the most ridiculous manner, such as beating with his foot, twirling his fingers and making sundry other contortions. All the while, an entire dependence was placed upon the real theatrical orchestra for concealing the imposture by their noise and skill.

In our manoeuvres of the stage we were very much assisted in comprehending the actors' directions by the interpretations of a French sea-officer, who had acquired the English language in a prison: he had apparently volunteered his services to the theatre for that night. Among the spectators we recognised several British officers; but I scarcely think they knew us in our new profession.

Preparations began now to be made for our final departure; several regiments had ere this time been despatched for America, and rumours were even afloat that that was our place of destination. The Spaniards and Portugueze who had enlisted in the British service were all dismissed: several of them belonged to our regiment. One Portugueze boy was allowed to remain, he having obstinately refused to leave us. The story of this youth is rather singular. In 1808, one of our officers hired him as a servant, and afterwards brought him to Glasgow, where the second battalion was quartered; here our hero, fired with military ardour, enlisted with it, and was latterly sent out in a draft to Lisbon, his native city. Previous to joining us in the interior, the officers had actually been obliged to use force in compelling him to visit his parents, who were both alive. Such was his ambition to be considered a 'Glasgow chap', that he was never heard to utter a syllable in either Spanish or Portugueze; in fact he had determined to renounce his country and make the headquarters of the 71st his home.

About this time, our honest Italian thought proper to decamp; he took his arms and accoutrements away, besides *borrowing* a watch from a sergeant. This odd character was afterwards seen in Paris by some 71st men;[11] he was then in the Prussian service.

On the 5th June we marched from Toulouse; a number of the inhabitants turned out to bid us farewell. It was soon found that the Italian was not the only deserter, – many men being missing; chiefly, it was supposed, from the attractions or enticements of French women; – no less than twenty of our regiment were in this predicament.

Our march to Bourdeaux occupied seventeen days: during the whole of our way we were delighted with the richness of the country, and, above all, with the kindness of the people; often did they refuse payment for provisions and wine: although some of them appeared to be in indigent circumstances, yet they were as bountiful as their more opulent neighbours. Sometimes we were quartered in splendid gentlemen's seats or châteaux, where, upon being ushered into fine carpeted rooms, with gilded beds, the natural diffidence arising from our total ignorance of such luxuries made us often draw back involuntarily; but the inhabitants generally succeeded in politely forcing us to make ourselves at home.

I am no would-be liberal, nor do I wish to chime in, for fashion's sake, with the present system of praising the French, in opposition to our old vulgar ideas of them; I only wish to state the truth, or, in other words, what I actually experienced. English, Scotch, or Irish hospitality may be talked of; I seldom if ever found any of it: it was in France that the true meaning of the word was realised to us.

After passing through Bourdeaux, we marched to Blanchefort camp, where a number of other regiments were waiting for vessels to convey them home. In addition to the good market which was established here, innumerable carts came out from Bourdeaux loaded with wine and brandy:

---

[11] The 71st was part of the Allied Occupation Army stationed in Paris after the defeat of Napoleon at the Battle of Waterloo in 1815.

their drivers kept up such an incessant noise in the camp, by the calling of 'Rhum', that sentinels were placed to prevent their entrance. By the word rhum, or rum; they intended that we should understand brandy. Frenchmen were not the only liquor-merchants; an Aberdeen smack having arrived; with a quantity of porter on board, – the 'pawky' crew came to the camp, and sold it at a franc per bottle, which was exactly the price of brandy; however, the muddy beverage was much run upon from its rarity.

In making a calculation of our numbers, it was found, that out of the 600 picked men who went to Portugal in 1810 only 75 remained. I do not mean to say that every individual out of this mighty deficiency was actually dead; some were in existence, but in a disabled state, although perhaps not just 'at the town's end for life'. In the month of July 1814, we embarked at Poliac in transports, and were conveyed to the mouth of the Garonne, where the whole regiment and two companies of the 50th, were put on board of the *Sultan*, of 74 guns. In the short space of five days the Cove of Cork was reached. Six precious years had elapsed since I left this place, in the company of 100 men, in the prime of youth. Of these, only three men and myself now returned![12]

---

[12] In his four-volume history of the Highland Light Infantry, *Proud Heritage*, Lewis Oatts calculated that only seventy-five men of the 652 rank and file who embarked for Portugal in May 1810 returned to Cork in 1814. No fewer than 340 Peninsular War veterans from the regiment were still alive in 1847 to apply for the General Service Medal. Ninety-three of them were awarded clasps for the Battle of Roleia (Roliça) in August 1808.

Appendix

Before and After

Although this book only covers the period between 1808 and 1814, the 1st Battalion of the 71st had been active against France since it declared war on Britain in 1793.

The 71st was in India when war broke out. It was sent to help capture the French fortress at Pondicherry but arrived after it had surrendered. Two years later the battalion's two elite flank companies were sent to Ceylon (Sri Lanka) where they helped capture several Dutch forts after Holland, as the Batavian Republic, sided with the French.

In 1798 the battalion was ordered back to Britain. The transfer of around 600 men to the 73rd and 74th Highlanders before sailing reduced the battalion to skeleton strength. In 1800 while stationed in Ireland the regiment was brought back up to its full establishment with a hefty infusion of volunteers from several Scottish home defence fencible units.

It was not until January 1806 that the 71st saw action again. It was sent to help capture the Cape of Good Hope on the southern tip of Africa from the Dutch. The 71st formed part of the British Army's first Highland Brigade and led the 72nd Seaforth Highlanders and 93rd Sutherland Highlanders in sweeping the Dutch aside at the Battle of Blaauwberg .

The 71st was then lent to the Royal Navy by the commander of the Cape expedition, Sir David Baird, a former commanding officer of the battalion, for an unsanctioned by London attack of Spain's colonies in South America. With the help of the St. Helena Regiment and some artillery, the 71st quickly overwhelmed the feeble force defending Buenos Aires in June 1806. Thirty men from the regiment on captured horses thwarted an attempt to spirit 600,000 silver dollars from the Rio de la Plata colony's treasury into the jungle interior. On the 10th August the approach of Spanish troops led to a popular uprising in Buenos Aires and the British were forced to surrender on the 12th August. It was not until September 1807 that the regiment was released from captivity.

The 71st's exploits after its return to Ireland until Napoleon's surrender in 1814 are recounted in this book. After a fresh round of recruiting, the 71st was earmarked for North America, where British and Canadian troops had been holding off an invasion from the United States since 1812. Unfavourable winds kept them at Cork until after a peace treaty was signed on Christmas Eve 1814.

Napoleon's escape from Elba in February 1815 saw the 71st on a war footing again. By then almost half of the 1st Battalion were new recruits. In late April they landed at Ostend and when Napoleon made his move in June, they were ready. The battalion marched for 36 hours with no food and few halts to reach Waterloo. They were posted behind the Chateau d'Hougoumont, along with the 52nd Light Infantry and eight companies of riflemen drawn from the 95th Regiment. The battalion suffered heavily during the initial French artillery bombardment of the British lines. By the time it moved to a more sheltered position between 60 and 70 men lay dead or wounded. The battalion's total losses at Waterloo were 67 killed and 144 wounded.

The 71st helped drive back at French infantry attack but then faced a series of seven cavalry attacks. It was while formed into a square that a single French cannon ball cut down 18 men. At one point the Duke of Wellington sheltered in the 71st's square. The battalion's coolness, discipline and steadfastness did much to keep the French from surrounding the key British defensive position at Hougoumont. When Napoleon sent his Imperial Guard forward, the 71st helped drive them back. Wellington then ordered a general advance and the 71st forced the Old Guard into retreat. The battalion over-ran an artillery battery and turned one of its cannon on the retreating French – claiming afterwards that they fired the last cannon shot at Waterloo.

Two days after the battle, the 71st mounted themselves on captured French horses and headed for Paris. The battalion was the only British unit allowed into the heart of the city and camped on the parkland alongside the Champs Elysees.

Selected Bibliography

Anon, *Memorials of the Late War,* Vol. 1, Edinburgh, Constable, 1828.

Anon, *Journal of a Soldier of the 71st or Glasgow Regiment, 1806–1815*, Edinburgh, William and Charles Tait, 1819.

Barnes, R., *The Uniforms and History of the Scottish Regiments*, London, Sphere, 1972.

Cannon, R., *Historical Records of the 71st*, London, Parker Furnival and Parker, 1852.

Edwards, P., *Talavera*, Ramsbury, Crowood, 2005.

Esdale, C., *The Peninsular War*, London, Penguin, 2003.

Flyer, A. E., *History of 50th (Queen's Own) Regiment*, London, Chapman and Hall, 1895.

Fortescue, J., *History of the British Army*, London, Macmillan & Co, 1899–1930.

Gavin, W., *Diary 1806–16*, Glasgow, Highland Light Infantry Chronicle, 1920.

Glover, M., *The Peninsular War*, London, Penguin, 2001.

——, *Wellington as Military Commander*, London, Sphere, 1973.

Goodspeed, D. J., *The British Campaigns in the Peninsular 1808–1814*, Ottawa, Queen's Printer, 1958.

Grattan, W., *Adventures of the Connaught Rangers*, London, Henry Colburn, 1847.

Greenhill Gardyne, C., *Life of a Regiment: The History of the Gordon Highlanders*, Edinburgh, David Douglas, 1901.

Haythornewaite, P., *Wellington: The Iron Duke*, Dulles, Potomac, 2007.

Hibbert, C., *Corunna*, London, Pan, 1972.

Keltie, J., *History of the Scottish Highlands, Highland Clans and Highland Regiments*, Edinburgh, A. Fullarton & Co, 1875.

Longford, E., *Wellington: The Years of the Sword*, London, Harper and Row, 1969.

Napier, C., *Battles of the Peninsular War*, London, John Murray, 1891.

Oatts, L. B., *The Highland Light Infantry*, London, Leo Cooper, 1969.

——, *Proud Heritage*, Vol. 1, London, Thomas Nelson and Sons, 1952.

Oman, C., *History of the Peninsular War*, Oxford, Oxford University Press, 1902–30.

Patterson, J., *The Adventures of Captain John Patterson*, London, T. & W. Boone, 1837.

Robertson, I., & Brown, M., *An Atlas of the Peninsular War 1808–1814*, New Haven, Yale University Press, 2010.

Snow, P., *To War with Wellington*, London, John Murray, 2010.

Sommerville, C., *March of Death*, London, Greenhill, 2003.

Uffindell, A., *The National Army Museum Book of Wellington's Armies*, London, Pan, 2005.